Full Circle

Reflections of a Romany psychic

Patrick Deadman

*Sometimes life brings you full circle to a place
you have been before just to show you
how much you have grown...*

TO Bz ALLAN

me o'd

X

GW00686323

Full Circle - Reflections of a Romany psychic

ISBN: 978-1-910181-50-8

First edition published in November 2017
Published in Great Britain by the Anchor Print Group Ltd

*This book is dedicated to the people I love,
past, present and future.
To my children, James and Katharine,
to my grandchildren Reuben and Beau,
and to my family and friends.*

It has been a pleasure to travel together.

*Special thanks to my dear friend, Andy Goss,
who helped give shape to my thoughts and commit
them to paper, and without whom this book would
not have been possible.*

*Thanks also to Holli Sheahan for the wonderful
cover artwork.*

Patrick Deadman

Contents

A period of darkness

Love, life and the universe

Full circle

Testimonials

"I know too well its truth, from experience, that whenever any poor Gypsies are encamped anywhere crimes and robberies occur it is invariably laid to their account, which is shocking, and if they are always looked upon as vagabonds how can they become good people?

I trust in heaven that the day may come when I may do something for these poor people. "

Extract from the 1836 diary of Queen Victoria

Introduction

It would be safe to assume that, like me, you too are amazed and fascinated by the man who seems able to look into every aspect of your life. As I write, I have had the privilege of knowing Patrick Deadman for more than 30 years.

Over those three decades both Patrick and I have known good times and bad. Yet one thing has remained constant for me: Additional insight to help guide, advise and reassure me along the way from a psychic counsellor I have come to call my friend.

I was a cub reporter working for a weekly newspaper in Leicestershire when first we met. I remember well that unexpected phone call at the office from a journalist friend of mine. She had met Patrick in a personal capacity in Derby and had been blown away by what he had related to her about her own life.

"Do you know Loughborough psychic Patrick Deadman? He is incredible," she gushed with enthusiasm. "You simply MUST do a story on him. He lives in your area..." And she passed on his phone number.

It was the beginning of my association with Patrick that has spanned six British Prime Ministers, the fall of the Iron Curtain, the launch of the World Wide Web, the first mobile phones and a seemingly endless series of conflicts across the Middle East...

Indeed, we live in a 'shrinking' but uncertain world increasingly reliant on technology. And yet the need for answers to age-old questions and a striving to connect spiritually remains as strong as ever, which is perhaps why Patrick remains so much in demand.

When we first met he was recently married, living in a small terraced house in Loughborough, where he worked long hours as a labourer at the Brush engineering factory. In his mid-twenties, he seemed an ordinary, friendly guy holding the same dreams for the future as anyone else.

Already he had learned to straddle two very different cultures. He had left behind his Romany roots and married a woman from outside the travelling community to settle in the Leicestershire university town and become a *Gorgia,* a house dweller, with the expectation of starting a family.

Yet the visions that had started as a young boy continued and Patrick would give professional readings on a part-time basis using the 'Gift' his Romany grandmother had helped develop in him. And his reputation across the East Midlands began to grow. But meeting the demands of a full-time labouring job and an increasingly busy client list was becoming impossible, and I remember him agonising over whether to focus full-time on his psychic work. Shortly after our first meeting he took that step – and has never looked back.

Life and its series of 'adventures' followed. For Patrick it brought the blessing of two beautiful children, James and Katharine, followed by a painful divorce. Suddenly, Patrick found himself having to juggle making a living with being a single parent of two young children.

In both key aspects of his life he has been successful, though the road has not always been easy.

He and I remained in touch, through thick and thin, sometimes collaborating on projects, including a series of ghost-hunting adventures across the East Midlands, taking in some of the most haunted spots in the land. His work has been interesting and varied, and has embraced paranormal investigations, exorcisms, media work, demonstrations - even supporting police investigations when all conventional methods had failed.

Professionally he is an established and respected psychic counsellor, with a client list which features the rich, the famous, the lost and the lonely; those who have found success and those who have not. And I guess that list includes you and I. He is known to thousands, through TV, radio and events he regularly attends across the country. Yet he remains as accessible as ever and personal readings are still the mainstay of his work.

He is in many ways the same earthy, charismatic and 'ordinary' man I first met in the mid-1980s.

Yet even today, Patrick remains something of an enigma to me, as he does to others.

On the one hand, a down-to-earth and generous friend.

On the other, a man who continues to surprise and mystify with a wisdom and sensitivity which, to be frank, does not seem of this earthly world.

Despite the many years I have known him the ability to explain, or understand how Patrick's remarkable 'gift' works still eludes me. How can he seemingly view our past, present and likely future with such remarkable insight and accuracy? And it is not just me. There are hundreds, if not thousands of people, from all backgrounds and walks of life that have been, and will continue to be, amazed by Patrick's work and the things he can 'see' about them. Even at distance.

I hope this book will help to understand and explain the life of one of England's leading psychic counsellors - and I invite you to join me through the following pages on what I am sure will be a remarkable and entertaining journey related in Patrick's own words.

His story as a psychic starts as a small Romany gypsy boy, who began to have powerful visions...

Now, with the experience and maturity developed over many years he is at the height of his success. But he remains determined to live a simple life in rural Leicestershire, close to the land and travel when he can, an urge that is never far from his thoughts. In this way he feels he is coming full circle to honour the traditions of the Romany way that is in his blood and is his culture.

Let's travel a while together!

Andy Goss, April 2017

Mum and Dad, very much in love

Early years

Chapter 1

Expectation was high for those who had gathered around the small white caravan pitched on the car park of the Horse and Coaches public house in the sleepy village of Abbot's Bromley. A baby boy was born to the Romany family who had been travelling through the Staffordshire area.

Yet celebration turned to immediate concern. The baby was sick with acute jaundice and the mother feared her first-born might not live to see the sun set that summer's day in August.

Mother and baby were rushed to the nearby hospital in Rugely where staff told the young Gypsy woman to fear the worst but hope for the best. After all, this was 1961. A Priest was called to administer last rites according to the mother's Roman Catholic faith.

As the holy man left he spoke to comfort the anxious mother.

"The boy will live," he assured her. "He has a job to do in life." And with that he left mother and baby and fate to take its course. The baby's name was Patrick.

But, of course, I did survive those first critical days in an incubator. I have since come to view every day of my life as a blessing; a bonus and tried to make the most of it. I wonder too what the Priest saw in the sickly scrap of humanity he prayed for that day at the hospital. Did he have a sense of my destiny? I wonder.

Not that I considered myself in any way different from anyone else as a young Gypsy boy, travelling in that small, white caravan the length and breadth of the country. They seemed blissful, carefree days spent in the company of extended family, with uncles, aunts, cousins and, of course, grandparents, who taught us the Romany ways. Often they told tales of great travelling adventures around camp fires to fuel the imagination, which is very much a Gypsy tradition.

My father, Joseph Deadman was one of four children who could still remember the days of the traditional horse-drawn *Vardo*, or bow-topped wagon that had been part of his parents and their parents' ways. It was perhaps where his love and knowledge of horses came from, so ingrained in the Romany lifestyle.

And yet by the early 1950s, when he was still a young man, those traditions were already disappearing, along with the freedom of the Gypsy peoples to follow their nomadic lifestyles as they had done for centuries.

My father was a full-blooded Romany, buying and selling scrap metal and pursuing all means of making a living that Gypsies can adapt to as they travel from one place to another. They included horse-dealing and breeding, and annual trips the famous Appleby Market Fair, where Gypsies still meet to trade horses and livestock. Or it might mean labouring for short periods, or hawking, going from house to house, offering to do odd jobs. And yes, laying tarmac driveways!

Joseph was by all accounts a handsome and resourceful man. Like many young Romanies at that time, he wore sharp, tailored suits and drove expensive cars. Olive skinned, slim, with dark hair and a golden tooth he had the look of a 1930s Mafia lieutenant, complete with wide-brimmed hat still fashionable at the time. He was a fine dancer too and not short of female Romany admirers. And, paying no bills and no taxes, he was always rich in cash.

My mother, Sabina, was a Scottish miner's daughter. With long, flowing black hair and a dark complexion she seemed more Hispanic than Celtic in appearance, with beautiful blue eyes. Although she had been raised in Bathgate, West Lothian, she had moved to the West Midlands to take up work as a secretary and short-hand typist in the bustling city of Birmingham. Like my father, she had many would-be suitors. Yet somehow romantic love never came calling.

When she met my father, it was love at first sight and he literally swept her off her feet at a local dance hall. Both were keen and accomplished dancers. She had learned the jive and the jitterbug from American GI's stationed in Scotland during and immediately after the war, and he had an instinctive sense of rhythm and movement. They must have made a handsome couple on the dance-floor. I think it must be where I inherited my enthusiasm for Rock 'n' Roll, my first love in popular music, encouraged as an infant by my mother, a keen Elvis fan. By all accounts, the pair quickly became inseparable. Both were already in their thirties, relatively late for the period to be unmarried. Perhaps it was meant to be. Certainly my father was Mum's first and only love.

Not that she was initially aware he was a Romany Gypsy. Nor did it seem to matter when she did find out. He could afford to wine and dine her like a 'lady' and he did. And she would have willingly followed him to the ends of the earth, which in a sense, she did.

She therefore did not hesitate to take up the travelling lifestyle when the time came. Besides, her family had known regular dealings with Romanies in Scotland, where her father ran a shop after he left the pits and he would sell to Gypsies in the area.

Granny Lizzie, my father's mother, who would become a great influence on my own life, explained to my mother she would have to adapt to Romany ways if she was to be accepted and happy. She was ready to do so and Granny Lizzie took my mother under her wing in what was to become a life-long friendship between the two women.

The wedding was, I understand, a grand affair as all Gypsy marriages – and funerals - are. My mother was accepted as part of the Romany community with scarcely the raising of an eyebrow, no doubt helped by her willingness to become part of it and her Gypsy looks.

And it was not unusual to marry outside the Romany culture, as my father had. Besides, my mother seemed a natural Gypsy and everyone seemed to agree the couple made a striking pair.

So began my mother's travelling days. From north to south, the length and breadth of the country they would travel by caravan from place to place as a community; an extended family; a nomadic people moving with the seasons, making ends meet by casual work or sometimes living off the land, as they had done for centuries. There was Uncle Roy, Auntie Lil and Aunt Birdie, a host of cousins and, of course Granny Lizzie.

With the travelling lifestyle came the constant challenge of change, adapting to new surroundings and of finding an income. But the sense of freedom!

And the choice to move on and travel again to a new place

when the urge was strong for new horizons, or the enjoyment of a particular place was gone, or the means of making a living was exhausted.

It was with such a sense of constant change that my childhood years were spent 'on the road'. I guess it is why there is a wildness and sense of restlessness in all Gypsy children that never leaves them. And why perhaps, the mind runs so free from the confines of a conventional upbringing.

Not that I realised my life was different from anyone else's in my early years. All I knew was the nomadic lifestyle of living in a caravan, with people I knew, loved and trusted, staying a while, then moving on when the 'time was right', like those around me. Wasn't everyone like that? I must have been six or seven when it first began to dawn on me that other people – other children – had different lives.

That was about the time I first went to school. It wasn't long after that I realised I was also different from the Gypsy children around me with the advent of my first psychic experience – a powerful and sudden vision that was to have a profound effect on me and reinforced in Granny Lizzie her long-held suspicion that I too had inherited the 'Gift'.

Chapter 2

There was a strong sense of falling through an empty void and a loud buzzing in the ears like an out of tune radio between frequencies. And there was a kaleidoscope of colour rushing passed me, which seemed all enveloping. At least in my mind, especially green. Different shades and consistencies of the colour green. It was confusing and totally disorientating. There was nothing to measure or gauge where I was, or what was happening. Nothing, except the continuing sensation of falling, the buzzing in my mind and the spectrum of colours all around.

That is the earliest memory I have and still remains vivid in my recollection. I have now come to believe the experience was real and comes from before I even took my first breath on that Summer's day in August, 1961. Yet as a young Romany boy, I did not consider myself to be in any way different, or unusual. That came later when I began gain a sense of myself and who I was within the Romany community – and that it was different from the house-dwelling *Gorgias* whom we so often relied upon for our existence as travelling people.

I would have been about eight, or nine years old when I became aware I existed as a person in my own right – and that I had the freedom to choose what I did, rather than what I was told to do. I guess that was the first awakening of a sense of self. And, yes, that I belonged to a different community from most people.

Not that there was in any way a sense that *we*, or *they* were inferior. Just different. And I was encouraged to believe there should be mutual respect between different communities and cultures. Besides, my father taught us to be tidy, especially before we moved on and I remember having to pick up sweet papers, even matchsticks before we were able to hit the road. He said we might be coming through again one day, as often we did and to leave things as we had found them. I can still see him telling me to look ahead – and to treasure what was good.

"We make a living from the *Gorgias*. So respect them and their ways." It was one of the best pieces of advice he ever gave.

But a different kind of travelling community disrupted the Romany respect for the environment and by the 1980s Irish tinkers and a ragtag collection of those seeking alternative lifestyles did not display the same ethos, bringing travelling people into disrepute with the communities they touched.

As for my father, he provided for us as well as he could. He worked hard, but he played hard too, which later led to his early decline and passing. Not many Romanies live to great age and my father was no exception. Yet my childhood recollections of my parents – and their relationship – remain relatively happy. Looking back, I know they loved each other and the life we had as a Romany family was sometimes hard, but often exciting and stimulating, despite the lack of regular schooling in my early years. Instead, I learned the traditional gypsy ways. As soon as you could walk and talk you were expected to contribute. There was a sense of community cohesion. A comforting sense of 'family' was always present, in good times and in bad.

I think my father's decline hastened when finally we gave up the travelling life. Perhaps there was something in him that died. Maybe he felt stifled and trapped by the confines of settled life so different from what he had known all his life. And the increased socialising and the drinking became a source of friction within our small caravan, certainly by the time we 'settled' on a caravan park owned by one of my uncles in Loughborough.

Yet memories of those early years of travelling have never left me, along with the sense, or perhaps even the need, to be free from convention – and to travel. There is a sense of the idyllic, of life without stifling boundaries 'on the road'. Freedom. At least as a child, without the worries parents and grandparents must have had about the constant challenge of moving from place to place and finding the means to source an income to provide for a young family.

Double trouble - my sister Sabina and I

I am convinced that the lack of regular schooling, rules and regulations allows the mind a certain freedom to develop that is now rare in our modern society. At least in the developed countries around the world.

Survival on a daily basis somehow made us more conscious of how precious life is, along with a closeness to the land and the value of basic necessities, which heightens the senses, living life a little closer to the edge than most. Certainly my Romany roots are a large part of who I am today.

My first experience of school would have been when I was six, or seven years old. We were staying at my Grandfather's house in Scotland, a large red-bricked terraced property. It was one of hundreds of cheap houses built for factory workers and miners in industrial heartlands across Britain fuelling the rapid growth and power of the European nations in the nineteenth and early twentieth centuries.

Grandfather Udi had left the pits and kept a small shop serving the local community. We visited often to see my mother's Scottish family and would sometimes stay for a prolonged period. On this occasion I recall I was very ill and had been suffering feverish hallucinations. I remember quite vividly 'seeing' the wind outside blow by from the window. Every strand and current of air was suddenly and magically visible to me in a whisper of shining strands rushing and swirling outside the house.

I remember too the look of concern in my mother's face as she comforted me through many hours and days of illness until the fever and the delirium left me. And then joy. I was presented with a box of brand new Matchbox cars, a rare gift outside the usual confines of birthdays and Christmases. Yet my blissful happiness and many hours spent racing, crashing and driving my cars on a series of adventures around the house was to be short-lived. As I began to recover, plans were already being made to send me to the nearby school as soon as I was well enough.

Unbeknown to me, my parents had decided that we would stay for a while in Scotland, not least of all because my father had regular work with Uncle Pat, my mother's brother after whom I am named, who ran a coal delivery business. Perhaps too, with the changing season and the onset of harsher weather, it had been decided to see it out before once more taking to the road.

In any case, my days without schooling were numbered. The authorities told my parents I had to be registered and attend. I didn't know what school was, but mother said I had to go.

Luckily I had Scottish cousins some years older at the same school and when the day came Uncle Pat's children escorted me there and were tasked with looking after me.

I guess that first day must have been confusing and traumatic. Certainly I was miserable. All the children spoke with a broad Scottish accent which I could not decipher. And the teachers did not seem overly interested in my sudden appearance. So I decided that schooling was not for me. After all, life had been fine so far without it. Besides, what possible use could it be for the travelling life we knew?! I figured my parents and Granny Lizzie could teach me everything I needed to know. Hadn't they always?

Being a Gypsy boy and crafty, with a new-found sense of self, as soon as break came on that first day and we were allowed into the playground, I jumped over the wall and ran all the way home to grandfather's shed. It became my daily routine. And there I would sit and wait, allowing my thoughts to wander, filling my mind with great adventures, eating my packed lunch when I became hungry.

Somehow I would amuse myself until school finished and as the children returned home I would join the procession as if returning from a whole day's study. It was an act I perfected and continued each day. And I got away with it for the duration of our stay! Even at the age of six, or seven, I had a strong sense of survival! By the time concerns were voiced about the absent 'Gypsy boy', we were already on our way...

It must have been around this time, when the memories of the dreadful Moors Murders were still fresh in the public's consciousness, that we were travelling once more southwards towards the West Midlands. The murders of the children, abducted, abused and buried in shallow graves upon Saddleworth Moor, Lancashire, had shocked and horrified early 1960s Britain. And who could not be familiar with the image of sinister peroxide blonde Myra Hindley and her partner Ian Brady with his vacant stare and twisted downturned mouth, oozing defiance and cruelty.

Lulled into a sense of joyous post-war prosperity which had finally taken hold and the upbeat optimism of the 'swinging sixties' here was a reminder that beneath the surface all was far from well. Hindley and Brady's romantic notion of being a modern-day Bonnie and Clyde was grotesquely twisted by the dark and callous cruelty displayed to their young victims, one of whom still lies buried undiscovered somewhere out on the desolate moors.

The morbid fascination for the crimes, which went hand-in-hand with the horror at the grisly revelations from the trial of 1966, is something which cast a shadow over the lives of every child born in the early part of the decade, heightened by the unprecedented media frenzy which somehow touched the lives of all those who lived through the period.

I remember we had spent many days travelling until we were back in the Cannock Chase area in Staffordshire, which we knew well and lies close to where I had been born. A place of outstanding natural beauty and once a Royal forest, the area has a sense of myth and mystery about it, dating back to the nineteenth century, with regular sightings of Black Dogs, Werewolves, big cats, even UFOs reported regularly over the last 150 years!

We were staying at an established Gypsy site with other families and children. But, being restless and mischievous, as I was, and wanting to stay occupied I took my little sister Sabina's hand and said to her in an excited whisper "Let's go and hide!" In an instant we were scampering off to conceal ourselves among some oil drums covered with a tarpaulin. And there we waited and waited, until our disappearance was noticed.

"Patrick... Sabina..." we heard our mother calling with an increasing sense of concern. "Patrick..." and of course, my excitement grew as I could see her from beneath the tarpaulin, though she couldn't see me. After a short while my mother's cries became more desperate and I realised that she was shouting that she could not find the kids and could everyone help look for them. The alarm raised across the camp, men women and children were suddenly searching for us, fanning out across a wide area to look for the 'missing' children.

As people were shouting and searching all around it suddenly occurred to me I had been naughty and that I had to escape to the familiar security of our caravan as soon as the opportunity allowed, dragging my hapless sister behind me. We scurried as fast as a 'long-tail' back to the caravan and hid in the cubby-hole where mother stored the blankets, our hearts thumping in anticipation of what might happen to us upon our discovery.

After what seemed an eternity, I heard voices outside the caravan and somebody enter. Footsteps approached. Peeping from the cubby-hole I saw the boots of a police officer, then my mother's feet and I heard her say she feared we had been taken, like those 'Moors' children. The boots of the policeman remained motionless and I heard him reassure my mother that he was sure we would be found soon. And then, as he stood surveying every inch of the caravan, the observant constable noticed the top of my head inside the hole in the corner. He calmly knelt down and looked straight at me, before gently, but firmly asking me to come out. He might even have smiled.

Hearing his voice and realising we had been discovered a sense of panic swept through me and I backed off into the darkest corner of the cubby-hole. Then I remember hearing the heavy step of of father's work boots approaching, as he was told we had been found. The constable stood up and the next thing I recall seeing was my father's face. He reached into the cubby-hole and dragged me by the scruff of the neck, pulling me into the light, my hapless sister attached to me.

A sense of doom overtook me, as I stood before the assembled group, head bowed, awaiting punishment, not daring to raise my eyes to look at my father. My mother was too relieved to be angry, but I remember being scolded by my father, whose deep frown I can still see. I wasn't beaten. But worse than that, at least for a Gypsy boy, I was kept inside for some considerable time and not allowed to go out. And then for some time after that, not to wander beyond the gaze of a trusted family member...

Chapter 3

The fair-haired boy with the impish grin stares from the framed black and white picture directly at me. The cheeky chappy is sporting the customary 'short-back-and-sides' of the period, still popular in the 1960s. I can see my mother in his face. But I see my father too. The shape of his eyes and the Romany contours of the face.

It's me, of course, aged about eight, or nine and my hair was to darken before I hit adolescence. A Gypsy boy. We are the product of our parents and it never ceases to amaze me how the genetic features of our forebears are reflected within us. I see my features and those of my parents in my own grandchildren. And so the cycle of life and the link to those who went before continues. It is who were are. Part of our identity, our heritage.

I see the same mischievous face in my grandson and I think to myself, there's a little Gypsy boy.

As for me when I was younger, mischief seemed my middle name. And, despite the scares along the way, my adventures were far from done. Even now! Our travelling days were, in a sense, a series of adventures that came with constant change of surroundings, bringing new challenges and experience. As I look back with fondness, I realise the sense of freedom from a nomadic lifestyle was something precious and shaped who I am today.

Growing up as a Romany child on the road was a way of life that seemed normal to me and I enjoyed the closeness to family and sense of community as we moved among those we knew and trusted implicitly. And I was, as yet, free from any awareness of my psychic sensitivity. Everything seemed 'normal' and part of natural life.

My first ghostly encounter came as a small boy during those travelling days, before we settled and before I started regular schooling in Leicestershire. We had been on the road for days. An eternity, or so it seemed to a young boy, confined in a small caravan. In any case, when finally we decided to pitch for a few days on the car park of a public house in the suburbs of a large town, there was suddenly an opportunity to escape and explore.

My mother had just popped out for a moment, perhaps to buy some provisions. "Let's go and find some toys," I said with a sense of excitement and off we went, my sister and I, towards what must have been the high street. And there it was. An empty, derelict house, whose front door was invitingly yawning open. In fact, there may not have been a front door at all.

It was an irresistible draw and in we went to explore. At the foot of the stairs inside, I remember looking up with a sense of foreboding. They seemed very steep and as Gypsy children we had never climbed stairs before, except for the one step into our caravan. And yet curiosity dictated we would climb those stairs, slowly, crawling on our hands and knees to discover what might lie on the upper floor of the empty house we had entered and seemed to be drawing us in.

At the top of the stairs there was a small landing and, to the left, a bedroom whose door was also open. Of course, we were curious to know what was inside. From the outside we could see remnants of broken, abandoned furniture and we wondered whether we might find some 'treasure'. As soon as we entered the bedroom the door suddenly slammed shut behind us with a frightening bang. The room turned ice cold, even though it was the height of summer and I felt an overpowering sense of danger.

The door seemed to have wedged itself shut and my sister began to cry as she watched my increasingly desperate efforts to open it. But it wouldn't budge. We were trapped! It seems strange now that I remained so calm, particularly as I could feel a growing sense of negative energy within the room, which seemed cruel, evil and angry. I seemed instinctively aware it wasn't good, and that we were not wanted there. And that we had to escape.

The room's front window was shattered and I realised it was our only avenue of escape. As my sister and I peered below with a growing sense of despair we could see our mother outside, who was shouting to us. "Come down, come down," she cried, unaware that were were trapped in the upstairs room. I felt we had to get out, as the feelings of negativity grew. Yet the window was our only route to safety.

"Let's jump," I told my sister as calmly as I could. I felt we had no other choice. And without any sense of fear at all, I held my sister's hand and we launched ourselves from the first floor window. I can still remember the sensation of falling... and then the safety of my mother's arms around me and we all fell backwards together onto the ground, as she cushioned our fall.

Miraculously, there wasn't a scratch on us, though my poor mother was black and blue for weeks to come.

Looking back, I believe there was a trapped spirit within that house, which did not want anyone there. It was powerful, angry and resentful. Even as a small child, I knew they weren't good feelings. The energy was bad and I felt we had invaded its space. It was one of my earliest experiences of the paranormal. But I had not been afraid. Somehow I had understood.

And the words of Granny Lizzie remain with me still.

"Don't ever be frightened of the dead – it is only the living that can hurt you." She was a remarkable woman and was to be a major influence on my life. And when the visions began to come she was there to reassure me and explain the 'Gift' she herself had inherited from her Romany forebears.

Though my ghostly experience in the abandoned house as a young boy was the first time I sensed a presence, my first vision of things to come occurred later and most unexpectedly. It was around Bonfire Night one year and I might have been nine, or 10. A big fire had been built to burn all the waste materials on the campsite.

All the children, myself included, were standing around the fire and I can still see the orange glow from the flames dancing on their excited faces as they were throwing various things onto it. It was my first experience of 'hearing' a voice in my head, an older person, definitely an adult. Initially I did not understand its significance, as I tried to make out what it was saying. Then suddenly the male voice shouted "Shut your eyes!" and being a young child I covered my face with my hands, just as a large explosion with a deafening thud threw me backwards.

A gas cannister, carelessly and stupidly had been thrown onto the fire, exploding, throwing out wood, rubber and other burning materials. My hair was singed and the backs of my hands burned. But my eyesight was saved. Some of the children were taken to hospital with facial burns and other injuries. But

I was unharmed. Somebody, or something had warned me about the impending danger BEFORE it happened. It is my first recollection of hearing a voice in my head and receiving a strong sense of things to come. And it had certainly saved me from injury.

Of course, voices speaking of future events, including strong images and feelings, have since become commonplace to me. And I have learned to interpret more clearly what I hear, see and feel over the years. Now I can control and channel those feelings, which helps me in the work I do. It is not about 'fortune telling'. It is about gaining a sense of past, present and future events in the lives of those who come to seek my guidance.

But that night around the bonfire was the start of it and alerted Granny Lizzie that I had indeed inherited the gift she herself had also experienced at a similar age decades previously. More visions would come as I grew older. But she was ready. I think she always knew. She just wasn't sure when it would start to manifest itself in me. When it did, the old lady was there to offer guidance and advice – and an insight that had been handed down over centuries. She was a truly wise and wonderful woman, who I feel watches over me still, though she passed away many years ago.

Chapter 4

It is said the Roma originated from Northwest India and began their nomadic life 'on the move' some 1,500 years ago, slowly migrating Westwards. Over the course of many centuries they made their way through Afghanistan and Persia, now Iran, travelling through the Middle East and into the Balkans. Eventually they reached Western Europe, somewhere around the beginning of the Tudor period, when the first Romany arrivals are documented. Exactly why and when they began their travels from the fertile lands below the Punjab is lost in the mists of time and was never recorded.

Some say they came originally from further north in India, from Kashmir and the southern sub-ranges of the Himalayas, perhaps remnants of those who had fought their way into India across the River Indus with Alexander and settled before eventually deciding to return to their point of origin. Not hard to imagine. Some of the northern peoples in the mountains are dark, but with lighter skin, sometimes with the most striking hazel, blue or green eyes. And even today many mountain tribes speak of distant links to ancient Greek conquerors to explain their apparent European characteristics.

One legend tells of a sixth century Persian emperor who was so distraught to hear that extreme poverty deprived his poorest subjects of music that he hired 10,000 *luris*, lute-playing men and women from northern India to travel and entertain the people across his dominions, rewarding them handsomely. When the musicians returned to his court a year later, 'hollow-cheeked' and hungry, having squandered the riches he had bestowed upon them, the king was angered. As punishment he banished the musicians from his empire to roam the world forever in penance...

Yet no written history exists and the Roma remain a people surrounded in mystery. It is the stuff of myth, legend and stories told around camp fires, handed by word of mouth from generation to generation. What is certain is their genetic ancestry scientists have recently traced back to India. And that seems to fit with some of the physical characteristics of the Roma, their dark skins and finely chiselled facial features, in addition to cultural aspects. Linguistics map a similar trail to the Indian sub continent and Romany language, which shares common vocabulary with Hindi and Punjabi, and other Indo-Aryan speech and dialects from the region.

Even the elaborate truck art of northern Pakistan which displays the same artistry with which the traditional bow-topped *Vardos* are associated, carved and painted with painstaking skill and pride might provide a cultural clue.

Certainly Granny Lizzie was a pure blood Romany. She looked more South Asian than European, with her dark skin, delicate facial features and hazel eyes, her hair pinned back, dressed in rich flowing fabrics for which Romany women have a fondness. She was petite in stature, but big on soul. As a Romany 'elder' she was respected. And she had a fearsome temper if crossed. Not even the wild Gypsy boys would dare upset her and were honour-bound by the Romany code to treat her with utmost courtesy – and a degree of awe. Besides, when fully riled she was a feisty match for any of them.

For me, Granny Lizzie's trailer was sanctuary. A haven of comfort and safety. I was her favourite grandson and spent many happy hours with her, often staying overnight in her trailer, away from the cramped conditions of our own small caravan. And she would entertain me with tales of her own travels, when the Gypsy peoples were free to roam, or tell bedtime stories of Shoshi the rabbit and Odgi hedgehog. Sometimes she would sing in a low, soothing voice; traditional Gypsy songs and lullabies passed from distant lands and times from when she was a young girl as I drifted off to a snug and comfortable sleep. They remain blissful memories.

And the cooking! There was always a black pot dangling from a tripod over an open fire outside Granny Lizzie's trailer from which the steam and smells of delicious stew would waft across the site. Strange how certain smells and aromas associate strongly with memories. Rabbit stew was a favourite. But her pigs trotters were out of this world and I can still taste the tender, sweet meat which would literally fall off the bone and the delicious stew blended from a rich variety of fresh vegetables laced with herbs as only Granny Lizzie knew how.

Sometimes there was food in abundance from the land. Snared rabbits, birds and hedgehogs. There were fresh vegetables and wild berries. And we would eat healthily and well.

Hedgehogs were seen as a treat and as the sun began to set we would hunt them out, setting off with sticks sharpened at both ends, and our dogs, or *jucks*, as the light began to fade and shadows grew long over the countryside.

The dogs would be sent into the hedges and bush rows to sniff out the hedgehogs, where we would be waiting, ready to spear them as they scuttled out. I can still hear them scream as they were pierced, crying out like small children, writhing, legs wriggling as they were skewered on our sticks. We would usually collect three, or four on our poles before darkness fell and head back to the campsite, holding the hedgehogs at arms length before us, as we knew they were full of fleas.

An open fire would already have been prepared for our return, serving as a beacon in the darkness. The hedgehogs, still alive and wriggling, were rolled in muddy water until they were coated (with mud) and then the hapless skewered animals would be roasted over the fire, turned until cooked evenly. I remember as a young boy watching the fleas jump from the hedgehogs, making tiny sparks dancing in the flames of the open fire. When cooked, my father would take a sharp knife and split open the creatures' underbellies like slitting a banana skin, exposing the meat, which we would tuck into, tearing at the delicacy with our fingers.

Hedgehog is delicious! Now that I am older I can describe the taste rather like game meat, such as pheasant. Many years later I met a chef who told me he had read in a traditional French cookbook that in the Middle Ages hedgehogs were once viewed by their Royal family and aristocracy as a rare delicacy! Besides hedgehogs, my father would also dress rabbits, hares and chickens and we all had our jobs gutting, skinning or plucking 'game' from an early age. In many ways it was a healthy, wholesome lifestyle, with fresh meat and vegetables often prepared on a daily basis.

Gypsy boys grow up fast. They learn the harsher realities of life young and are taught as children how to survive – and to play their part within the community. Strength in family and identity. It is part of the Romany code.

One of my earliest memories is of going to 'work' with my father, almost as soon as I could walk, knocking on people's doors as he sought a day's labour, clearing gardens, or odd jobs. Sometimes we would push leaflets through doors, asking for any unwanted scrap iron, to be collected the next day. Or we would go 'hawking' from door-to-door, selling assorted wares the family had come by.

Respite for me was Granny Lizzie's trailer. Aside from the black cooking pot hanging over the open fire and her famous stews she was equally renowned for the 'Gift' as a respected 'seer'. Often I would watch her bent over her cooking pot checking her stew, wooden spoon in hand. And as folk passed by she might greet them warmly and confide an intimacy, luring them into her trailer with the promise of further revelations of the experiences that had touched their lives – and of those yet to come.

Her reputation was such that people would travel the length and breadth of the country for a reading with Granny Lizzie. But forget the stereotypical crystal ball fortune teller with head scarf and sovereign earrings. She was above that and possessed a natural gift. She could read someone intimately just by looking at them. It was all there to see, the images, the feelings and the overpowering sense of someone's very being. It is the same for me today, although watching my grandmother at work, as I sometimes did, I never could have guessed I would follow so closely in her footsteps, even though she foresaw it many years before I even had my first psychic experience. I can hear her still, as she looked into my eyes and said: "Watch me well, for you will be doing as I do one day." And she would smile knowingly, showing the creases of age and wisdom in her face.

For light relief she watched the wrestling on her black and

white TV, which she adored with a passion and enthusiasm which amuses me still. Man mountains like 'Giant Haystacks' and 'Mick McManus' were up there as her heroes. And if she perceived any 'cheating' or foul play she would unleash a barrage of earthy swearwords as only Romanies know how! There was such life and passion in my grandmother, along with an experience of traditional Romany ways fast disappearing I found intriguing and comforting. Above all, I knew she loved me and that I loved her. Time with Granny Lizzie was always wonderful and inspiring.

Early 20th century Romany family

Yet unbeknown to me, her days were already numbered. Not that she ever complained about her health. Not even the crippling arthritis in her hands which so troubled her.

It all seemed to happen when finally the family accepted our travelling days were over and we were offered an opportunity to pitch long-term on my uncle's campsite in Loughborough. New legislation had restricted the travelling Romany lifestyle further, often putting us in breach of the new laws. Pitching anywhere, even the traditional stops frequented by Romanies for generations, now carried the constant risk of being served with eviction notices and falling foul of the law.

The exploits of certain non-Romany travellers in upsetting communities hadn't helped, reinforcing long held prejudices and suspicions against the Gypsy peoples. It was the end of the road, which many had seen coming for many years. Not that I knew it at the time. It was just another campsite and I did not know how long we might be staying, or that life, as I had known it, would change so dramatically.

At first life within the Leicestershire university town was good. And yet as weeks became months they seemed to mark a change in my father and hasten his decline. It was as if something was dying within him. He compensated for the loss of the freedoms he had known all his life and the closeness to the land by taking an allotment along the canal, where he kept an assortment of animals: Chickens, ducks, geese, rabbits and our pet donkey, 'Tony'. And for a while it seemed to help. But it wasn't to last. Within the course of the year our lives were to change forever beyond all recognition.

Chapter 5

The moment I climbed into my father's van I knew something was terribly wrong.

I'd had a good day at school, which I had started within a few weeks of our arrival in Loughborough. My mother had told me I would have to go, as I had in Scotland, so already I had been contemplating an escape plan. But she was one step ahead and escorted me daily to the gates of Cobden Junior School. Yet this time it was different. The first positive was that I could understand what the other children and the teachers were saying! And everyone seemed friendly. At least until they found out I was a Gypsy, living in a caravan.

But this day was particularly upsetting when my father picked me up after school and I climbed onto the seat beside him. I noticed he was crying. As I looked at him enquiringly, he began sobbing uncontrollably. It was especially shocking to me, as it was the first time I had ever seen my father display such emotions. Anger and frustration, yes. Even violence. I'd seen that before. But not this. My immediate thoughts were that there had been a family bereavement. As my mind raced, wondering who might have died and my own eyes began to moisten I heard my father's trembling voice say: "Tony's dead."

Tony, the donkey! I breathed an inward sigh of relief as my father began to cry again. Sad though it was, I was simply glad it was not a member of our family that had died.

But I was confused by the strength of emotion I was witnessing in my father as I watched the tears roll down his cheeks. It never occurred to me he felt a closeness, or an attachment to animals, having seen him so often 'neck' chickens and rabbits in front of our eyes without a flicker of hesitation or regret. But Tony was different. The animal was something we kids could ride on and to my father, a significant symbol of his Gypsy identity that he clung to when our travelling days came to an end. That was what the whole allotment setup was about. In my father's mind it was a way of keeping animals that had been part of his life from his earliest memories of life on the road.

As for poor Tony, his harness had been left on and had somehow become tangled in the allotment fencing as the animal had desperately twisted and turned in his bid to free himself, only to tighten the leather like a noose around his neck.

The result was therefore inevitable and my father had found him asphyxiated, hanging from the fencing. The loss was devastating to him. And to compound the agony my father felt in seeing a last, desperate link to the life he had known so cruelly taken, Mr Fox visited the allotment the following week, killing every chicken, every duck and goose we possessed. It was a hammer blow.

Soon afterwards my father decided to give up the allotment and, looking back, his drinking habits started to become more regular after that. As a mature adult myself now, I can understand what a personal torture and disappointment he must have felt with how his life had turned out. He drank more and suffered prolonged bouts of depression, which would sometimes lead to explosive outbursts of anger and to fights, inside and outside the caravan. And I remember thinking this was not how life should be.

Instead of viewing our caravan as a place of safety and security, I was now only too happy to escape and attend school, especially as it was so much less daunting than my first experience in Scotland. It seemed much more welcoming. Initially no-one knew my background. Besides, there were toys and games I had always dreamed of that were suddenly available to me in-school, but which had always been beyond the means of my parents. There was also an opportunity for the first time to participate in arts and crafts – and to paint – allowing me to express my artistic side for the first time. And there were school dinners, including my favourite: Cheese and onion pie, with roast potatoes and plum tomatoes. So school wasn't so bad after all. I therefore no longer had any intention of running anywhere, except, perhaps, to school. My father said I looked like a 'proper *Gorgia*' in my white shirt, grey pullover and trousers as I prepared to leave the caravan one morning.

I even made my first friend: Paul Midgely. I called him 'Piggy', because of his upturned nose; he called me 'Concorde' in return, due to my extended Romany nose. I think it was my first association with a *Gorgia* boy and I remember I was desperate to be liked. He was an Arsenal fan, so I followed suit, even though I knew nothing about football. And I began to listen to the football results on the radio, much to the surprise, perhaps even dismay of my father, who viewed the sport as something followed by *Gorgias*. It wasn't the Gypsy way.

The only sports of any interest to Romanies seemed to be boxing, or perhaps horse-racing!

But I wanted to be accepted at school, where I was the only Gypsy boy. So football became my passion, as it is to this day, following the fortunes of the 'Foxes', my beloved Leicester City Football Club, where I am the proud owner of a season ticket.

But as the days passed school suddenly didn't seem so much fun any more. The play element became less as we began to focus in earnest on the essential and inevitable three 'Rs', reading, writing and arithmetic. Having missed so much schooling in my early years all the other children were way ahead of me. My difficulties were compounded by the fact that I was left-handed and made harder still by my dyslexia, which was only diagnosed as I grew older and hardly recognised, or understood at the time as an obstacle to learning.

Yet still school held a certain magic for me. Along with the mystery of education, whose opportunities I desperately wanted to unlock, I was enthralled by the stories that were read to us at the end of each school day, like 'Robinson Crusoe', or 'The Lion, the Witch and the Wardrobe', which fired my imagination and drove me on to want to learn to read, which I finally did. But still to this day I have not mastered the elusive and confusing art of spelling! I was simply so far behind the other children, who already knew their alphabet and their basic times tables.

And then it was discovered I lived in a caravan. I was a Gypsy. Children can be cruel and I remember being taunted relentlessly. Gypsy! Gypsy Boy! Dirty, thieving Gypsy! As the eldest of my contemporaries within our family group, I had no other siblings, or cousins at school. Suddenly I seemed alone. Even 'Piggy' kept his distance. So often I found myself in my own company. Not knowing how to read and write added to my sense of isolation. Now at breaktime I began to regard the playground walls, which were very high, like a prison and longed once more to escape. But how to possibly scale those walls without the use of a ladder?

While the other children played I pretended to have friends, creating imaginary playmates running together and chasing each other. But in reality, no-one would play with me and instead would try to bully me and call me names. I just wanted to make friends and for children to like me.

School portrait

Granny Lizzie

My first feelings of rejection! And I felt I would never be accepted by the *Gorgia* community, which seemed a world apart and which might never be bridged.

At the same time life in the caravan was also becoming increasingly difficult, with the recent arrivals of my brother Joseph and sister Lilian. Now we were two adults and four children in a confined space, almost sleeping on top of each other. A council representative came to call, took one look at the cramped conditions we were living in and an offer of a council house soon followed. The three-bedroomed terraced house in Duke Street was, ironically, just a stone's throw from our caravan on the very corner of the site on which we had been living.

Downstairs the house had a front living room, a back room, also a kitchen and bathroom. It was the first time I had ever seen a bath and shower unit! This was like heaven. Never had I seen so much living space – and that was just the ground floor. Upstairs was another entire dimension to me: My own room, equipped with a double bed all to myself. There was even an attic room which, as it turned out, no-one would sleep in. Even my father said it felt 'bad'. The room was haunted. But that's another story. Suddenly life seemed to have improved dramatically. And yet what was to be the worst moment of my young life was approaching...

Chapter 6

The sombre cortège stretched as far the eye could see, snaking slowly along the country road towards the township. At the front, sweeping black limousines, followed by a ragtag collection of cars, trucks, even trailers of almost every description formed the extended column as it then made its way through the town towards the small church. Some said it was over a mile long, swelled by the Romany community from far and wide – some from overseas - who came to accompany the old lady on her final journey and to pay their last respects.

I was numb and literally sick with grief. It was the first time I had experienced a family bereavement and the sense of loss was profound. As I stepped from one of the lead vehicles and stood with my family gazing at the hearse before us, I could hardly believe that I would no longer be able to enjoy the company of my grandmother. Granny Lizzie was gone from my life. As I stared at the coffin it was hard to imagine that she was confined within that small wooden box and that I would never see her again in this world.

I had not foreseen Granny Lizzie's passing. It had not even occurred to me that she would not always be there and that she had become increasingly frail. As a boy I took for granted she might be a comforting part of my life forever. But here was a stark reminder that things change. Nothing remains the same, neither good, nor bad. It seemed a hard lesson. And I felt guilty. Guilty because since moving into the house on Duke Street I had no longer visited her often, especially as I was going to school full-time. In fact, I had not seen my grandmother for several weeks before she died, something I regret to this day. We therefore never had a chance to say goodbye. But perhaps that was meant to be. Because in some ways she remains part of my life still and I have always sensed she is with me in times of trouble.

My father had gone to visit her in her trailer on the nearby campsite. He knew how ill she was. But he had not spoken of his own concerns for her. I think he too was surprised by the speed of her sudden decline and passing. He returned home from the campsite that day sombre-faced and we immediately knew something terrible had happened as soon as he stepped inside.

"Granny Lizzie... she's gone," he announced ashen-faced in a low voice thick with emotion.

At first I couldn't quite take it in. I suppose children don't. It was unreal; a bad dream. And then there were tears and family hugs as we sought to comfort each other.

Preparations for the funeral were almost immediate. My father said we would make sure Granny Lizzie would have a send-off spoken of for years to come and befitting her status as a respected 'elder' within our community. He may have said the usual things people say when they struggle with the concept of loss: That she would still be looking down on us; that she would continue to live in our hearts and in our memories. But his words washed over me. I was totally numb with shock. I still did not want to believe I would never again be spending time with my grandmother in her trailer.

My father said we were all to look our best for Granny Lizzie's funeral, so I was measured up for my first suit. Indeed, we all looked very smart in our made-to-measure outfits. And yet, perhaps ironically for a Gypsy, I became travel sick! Perhaps it was the overwhelming diesel fumes from the many vehicles assembled for the slow-moving cortège that overwhelmed me. Or perhaps I was sick with grief. In any case, I remember vomiting in the limousine all over my new suit, which only added to my sense of misery that day. They cleaned me up as best they could, but I remember being conscious of the sickly smell which clung to me and feeling very unwell. It was without doubt the worst day of my young life.

Looking back, I don't think I wanted to believe it was happening. Most people are probably the same. It wasn't until I stood staring at the hole in the ground they were to place my Granny in that the reality of that loss – the acceptance of it – began to dawn on me. Yet I was not alone in my grief. Those standing with us in our loss must have numbered many hundreds, most of them people I had never seen before, resembling a football crowd united in sadness and silence as my grandmother's coffin was lowered into the ground.

Images of her wizened face, her soothing voice and the comfort her trailer had provided me in the early years of my life came into my thoughts, as they still do.

And in my mind I was back in her trailer on the bed, surrounded by her prized Crown Derby porcelain collection and shining brasses, sipping a mixture of sherry and raw egg yokes she would make to ensure I slept soundly, as I always did.

Then there were stories of when she was a girl and roamed free, and of expansive, lush green meadows, tending horses and small livestock that moved along with the bow-topped wagon on their travels. Of her father, making a simple living from iron mongery, polishing and sharpening knives on his grindstone as the sparks flew. They were magical stories which I took into my dreams as I slipped into a deep and satisfying sleep. They gave me a sense of who I was and a pride in my Romany heritage.

She was my earliest inspiration and gave me the strength to get through the toughest times, not least of all because I knew she truly loved me. And her faith in me instilled a confidence and a sense of identity in me. She also guided my first steps in developing the 'Gift' from the time my first psychic experiences began to emerge, giving them sense and meaning. And she provided reassurance. Above all, she showed me the way as I began to take my first psychic steps. Of course, seeing such a naturally gifted psychic at work also helped me accept as 'normal' the powerful forces when they began to flow through me with increasing strength as the years passed.

I had watched her work many times, leaving the people she read with a sense of awe and amazement with what she told them about their dearest, deepest experiences and of their darkest fears, their brightest hopes, their fondest dreams.

"Patrick, one day you will be doing this. Take notice," she had often said. There was no doubt about it. She knew. She saw it. Looking back, I suppose the very fact that possessing an ability to 'see' and read people was not seen as abnormal within the Romany world was a big factor. To accept the ability and not to be afraid to embrace it; that it was a normal and natural thing, which those outside the Gypsy community were largely ignorant, sceptical, or even fearful of.

So she set me on my way. She was my first mentor.

Mum with Sabina and Lilian

But it would be some years before my own psychic powers would take a further step forward and another remarkable woman was to come into my life to help me develop the talents which were yet to be fully awakened and properly channelled.

I regard the immediate months and years following Granny Lizzie's death as something of a psychic void. Besides, the focus was very much on school life – and surviving the daily challenges and prejudices that lay ahead as I struggled to be part of the *Gorgia* world I did not yet fully understand or feel part of. Certainly my grandmother's death was my first loss of somebody I loved so very much.

Garendon High School was a further change. A bleak and barren time for me. The lessons were harder. The sense of isolation and marginalisation more profound. I loved history and art, which some teachers recognised. And as I grew older I was able to excel in sport. But the bullying was intense and my sense of misery grew as the initial magic I had held about education began to ebb into painful drudgery, punctuated by prejudice and abuse.

There seemed no release. Hopes of unlocking the opportunities that education might provide slipped away as I began to fall further behind the other youngsters who seemed to have every advantage to help them. The sounding of the final bell signalling the end of the school day was therefore a daily release. Those pre-teen years were a time of confusion to me. Perhaps they were transitional, but they were painful. I was a Romany Gypsy, but I was not. Nor was I part of the *Gorgia*, house-dwelling world I longed to be accepted by at school. It was to be a dark period in my childhood in which I sought to affirm my identity – and a far cry from the happier, carefree days of life on the road as a young boy, when I was more certain of my place and my sense of community.

A door opens

Chapter 7

It started the very first day at Garendon High School. A group of older boys approached me at break-time and demanded my dinner money. Instantly alert to the possibility of a fight I felt the adrenaline rise. Instinctively I sought an escape route, but there was none. The boys were older, stronger and no doubt faster. And not a teacher in sight. I realised almost immediately with a sudden sense of doom I would have to fight.

Most Gypsy boys know from an early age how to make a fist! Some fancy their chances and go on to take part in bare-knuckle fighting, something of a sporting obsession among the Gypsy peoples. My father had always told me to strike hard and fast. And first. Squarely on the jaw. The boy who spoke to me and demanded I hand him my cash was bigger and brasher than his friends who surrounded me. I remember the anger rising in me when I thought about them taking my dinner money from me and the injustice of it. I thought again about my father and without further hesitation I took his advice and slammed my fist onto the older boy's jaw...

The blow was totally unexpected and he reeled backwards and fell to the floor. And I was on top of him, punching his face repeatedly. But inevitably, he was able to wriggle free and overpower me. Suddenly he was bearing down on me with a vengeance. Not that I felt his blows. And thankfully the commotion had finally attracted the attention of a teacher, who pulled the bully off before he was able to give me a real beating – and we were both marched to the headmaster's office. I explained what had happened and admitted I had punched the older boy to protect my dinner money. Mr Ferrigan listened carefully with knitted brow, sighed deeply and slowly shook is balding head. I was lucky. He believed my story, helped no doubt by the fact the older boy was a known bully and I escaped any punishment. At least on that occasion.

As the bully and I were ushered out the headmaster stopped me and said: "Deadman, I don't want to see you in this office again. Is that clear?" I nodded sheepishly and left, the bruising on my hands and face beginning to throb. But the story spread. And no-one picked a fight with me again at Garendon. Not in three years.

I had decided to add to my fighting mystique by telling my classmates that I was related to one of the greatest fighters of all time: Bartley Gorman, self declared *King of the Gypsies* and undefeated bare-knuckle boxing champion of Britain and Ireland. Gorman was said to be a cousin of my father's, although such is the stuff of family myth and I may never know the truth of it. What is not disputed is the man's incredible fighting prowess which has never been equalled. Legend has it he was inspired by seeing a newsreel of a young Cassius Clay fighting in 1960 and modelled himself on the black fighter, adopting a similar style in the bare-knuckle arena. It paid off, with Gorman undefeated in scores of fights across the country over the next 40 years, until his retirement in 1997. He was even to meet and spar with his hero when the then Mohamed Ali visited the UK. Certainly Gorman was to the Gypsy peoples what Ali was to Black Americans.

Not that I had any aspirations to have a reputation as a fighter at school. I just wanted to be left alone by the bullies. And it seemed to work. Yet the isolation and the prejudice continued and I went largely without real friends for the duration of my high school years, continually mocked and insulted for my Gypsy background, feeling I didn't really belong. I found no release in the lessons, with which I struggled to keep up. It was a confusing and lonely time in which I found little solace, except in history and art, for which I had a natural flair.

At the age of 13 my high school days were finally over. Often regarded by children as the happiest days of their lives, free from impending teenage angst, mine had been miserable. And still I could barely read and write when I started at the upper school. Nor did I really feel I fitted in with the Gorgia community, even though we had been living within bricks and mortar for several years and our nomadic travelling lifestyle seemed no more than a distant dream.

Yet it was at Burleigh College that my life took a turn for the better. The catchment area for its students was wider. There were black and Asian youngsters from Loughborough who endured similar prejudice and an alienation from their own cultures, which somehow drew us together. It was almost like segregation. The white kids would sit one side of the class, the black and Asian boys and girls on the other, barely interacting, often trading insults. And I felt in the middle, unsure which side I should be on.

In the event it was to be the South Asian community with which I felt an affinity, which led to my first firm friendship with a Punjabi boy. And for a while we were almost inseparable.

We even took up Karate together, something I found I had an aptitude for, going on to become an East Midlands junior champion. So perhaps there is some of that Gorman fighting blood in me after all! I found the required control of mind and body as fascinating as I enjoyed the martial art's physical demands. And the coordinated disciplines needed have stood me in good stead throughout my life.

Joining the club allowed me to mix with young people of all backgrounds who shared a common passion. What's more, my own background didn't seem important. No-one really seemed interested. It didn't matter where you came from. It wasn't relevant. So for the first time I felt accepted for who I was. And that was an important step in my young life, further spurred by finding something I was good at which did not require any kind of education. We were all there to learn from scratch. It was a level playing field and I was able to excel on my own merits. Above all, I believe Karate was a great release for the frustrations I had felt during my time at school.

After initial rejection as a young child due to my Romany Gypsy background I had tried very hard to adapt and pretend to be a *Gorgia* to be accepted. Acceptance. Isn't that what we all strive for? To be liked. Certainly not to be judged and shunned. So looking back I think I had learned to hide my true identity in a bid to gain that sense of acceptance – and to be like the other children. Now, suddenly, with my success at Karate, I began to receive recognition, even respect for the first time since our travelling days had ended, and my confidence began to grow.

Throughout my high school years at Garendon and into my early teens my psychic visions were rare. In this spiritual sense, as I have said, following my grandmother's death, there was something of a void. Yet Granny Lizzie did still come to visit in my dreams, which were very vivid and real. I felt she really was with me and would bring with her an overwhelming sense of love which surrounded me, which made me feel secure. That aside, I had moments of intuition, of psychic experience and occasional visions. But there was nothing profound.

Nor was there any sense of psychic development during what had been in many ways a very bleak and lonely time in my life, with very few friends. But that was about to change.

The dreams in which my grandmother came to me became stronger and more frequent. In addition to her smile and the sense of comfort she brought was a new degree of assurance she seemed to be wanting to relate to me. "Believe in yourself," she would tell me. "If you don't, no-one else will." The increasing frequency of the dreams in which she appeared seemed to coincide with the desperate levels with which I tried to deny my own Romany roots. I longed to escape the prejudice and the bullying I had experienced from such an early age from the *Gorgia* community. So in this sense, I was unsure of my own identity, which I am now sure my grandmother was urging me not to abandon.

It was around this time, when I was still struggling to come to terms with who I was and where I came from that my Romany background unexpectedly opened a new door, which was to lead me to the true awakening of my spiritual self and allow my psychic abilities to develop. The boy's name was John. He approached me one day and asked me directly: "You're a Gypsy aren't you? My mum says you people are supposed to be psychic. Aren't you supposed to believe in spirits?" I remember being quite shocked, as *Gorgia* folk tended not to speak about such things openly, least of all of anything that might be of interest about the Romany way.

He told me his mother was a spiritualist and that she would

like to meet me sometime. So I answered that he was right that some Gypsies had the 'Gift' and told him proudly about Granny Lizzie and the remarkable talent she had to read people. And a new friendship was born. Within a few days an invite came via John from his mother, Gill, to drop by for a chat. It was to prove a pivotal moment. The family was more liberal and freer in thought than most, not entirely dissimilar to Romanies. And they were interested and engaged in spiritual questions. I felt comfortable there from the very first meeting and was to become a regular visitor to John's family, where I was the centre of interest, rather than shunned for who I was.

John also had two brothers who became close friends. It was like I became a part of the family, able to pay a visit anytime, like a second home and where I was made genuinely welcome. And that extended to the boys' mother, Gill who in time was to become the second big influence in my development as a psychic.

She helped awaken my 'third' eye, teaching me about opening my chakras, and how to channel what I saw and felt psychically. It was to be the beginning of a new and exciting phase in my life. Above all, she gave me confidence, assurance and encouragement to take those important next steps in my development. They were to have a profound effect on my life. And never would I see things in the same way again...

Chapter 8

The woman who opened the front door seemed to radiate warmth, openness and compassion. I could hardly have guessed then the influence she was to have on the course of my future, or that we would become such good friends. Gill looked into my eyes and smiled.

"So nice to see you Patrick," she beamed. "John's told me all about you. Come in, come in..." and I stepped inside. Thinking about it now I realise it was like a new door opening in my life. It was the start of a beautiful friendship. Not that I could have known that then. But somehow I did sense meeting Gill was going to have a big impact on my life. And she did in the most remarkable, unselfish way imaginable.

I remember being a little anxious on my way to John's house that first time to meet his mother. Yet the moment I saw her my nerves disappeared. She had this way about her which allowed people in her company to relax immediately. She emanated kindness and unconditional love. It was clear to see in her face, from her generous smile to the warmth that shone from her eyes. She was small and blonde, a little stout and, I guess quite 'motherly'. Yet she was still strikingly attractive, even to a 14-year-old youngster, as I was then, though she would have been in her early forties at that time.

She was excited to meet me, she said and had heard all about me from John. She was genuinely interested in my Romany background and I remember even that first time we spoke about spirituality and I told her all about Granny Lizzie. She was open and receptive. And I must have basked in the attention, which was all positive and accepting of my Gypsy culture, which she admired and wanted to know more about. I wasn't used to that. She told me she used to play with Gypsy children when she was a little girl and that they realised then their way of life was disappearing. She even knew some Romany words and terms – and I remember being fascinated to hear them from a *Gorgia's* mouth! There seemed an instant bond between us.

In addition, she not only accepted what I related about Granny Lizzie and my own psychic experiences, such as they were at that time, but she wanted to know more about my life as a Romany Gypsy boy and what it meant to me.

She also told me about her own experiences and her involvement in spiritualism - and what she had come to believe. But there was nothing forced. It all seemed very natural and went hand in hand with the friendships I had developed with John and his siblings – and their family life, which I began to feel a part of.

In the days and weeks ahead I was a frequent visitor at John's house. And, of course, I would see Gill too. And it wasn't long before she asked if I would like to come along to the spiritualist church in Loughborough. I accepted the invite, not least of all because I was curious to meet people who might be spiritually enlightened and from whom I might learn and develop. Since my grandmother's death I had not come into contact with anyone who might help me explore my spiritual side... and I had been having some powerful psychic experiences which I hoped I might come to understand

Although I was excited about the prospect of going to the

spiritualist church, I didn't really know what to expect. Yet I figured if Gill was a member of the church, it could only be a good thing. The reality was that I didn't know anything about spiritualism at that point. The only church I knew was the Catholic Church, which I attended every Sunday with my mother, who held a strong belief. My father was an atheist, even though he wanted us to be brought up as Roman Catholics. He would drop us all off in his van and my mother would escort us to church for Mass, while he drove off to the local pub. That was my father's only true 'church', right up to the end.

So although I was keen to meet other people with spiritual knowledge I felt I was being disloyal to my own church – and particularly to my mother's beliefs. I was certain she would disapprove, which in fact, she did. But I felt I had to go anyway and I placed my faith in Gill, whom I felt I now knew well enough and trusted. She was a naturally gifted medium, very different from my grandmother. She seemed kind, patient and giving. Above all, she was genuinely interested in helping me to take the next steps in developing my psychic ability. I was also pleased that John was coming along too. But it was new territory for me. The spiritualist church was created to prove existence beyond physical death and its mediums communicated with those who had passed on, with the help of spiritual guides and to receive insight about the living.

A medium would always conduct the service, which would include prayers and often talks on philosophy. I saw incredibly talented mediums at work, creating awe and amazement in the things they could reveal to those attending. Their talent inspired me and I wanted to learn more; I wanted to know how they worked and channelled the images, the voices and the feelings they experienced. I wanted to learn their techniques.

I was intrigued and fascinated. Having attended several services, I remember seeing one incredibly talented medium in particular who truly was breathtaking. His name: Gordon Higginson, who was renowned across the UK and Europe and known as 'Mr Mediumship'. Although his reputation was dogged by accusations of fraud, I believe his abilities were genuine. When I saw him demonstrate his remarkable gift, he was able to go to anyone, tell them all about themselves, what they did, where they lived – even what they had in their pockets! I was truly impressed as a youngster by what I witnessed and how he interacted with his audience through his mediumship, which created a lasting impression on me. At the time, the man inspired me like no other.

It wasn't long before Gill – and others – suggested I attend the local spiritualist development circle to move my own abilities forward. I was delighted and flattered. And I saw this as an opportunity to learn and progress. I was happy that John also attended. We were the youngest among the group, most of whom were middle-aged, or elderly and had been involved with the spiritualist church for many years. The circles were run by different local mediums. We would sit literally in a circle and close our eyes and the medium would seek to link with their spirit guide. When the medium began to speak, it would usually be in a different, alien voice, which would sometimes make John and I want to giggle. So I guess we must have held a degree of scepticism. Or perhaps it was simply that, although I was fascinated by the people I came into contact with, a sense was beginning to form within me, that this wasn't quite the direction I wanted to take.

But I stayed with it. That is not to say spirits don't come to me in my work, but mediumship is not my everyday calling.

I have focused my work on the living, leaving mediumship to people who specialise. Yet Gill had become a good friend and offered me her own insights and advice. She seemed more open to encouraging to wider development.

I think she knew that was the way forward for me. She was also a natural healer and knew about energy centres. She taught me the techniques which would help me to open my chakras, including my 'third eye' to visualise and the solar plexus to feel and channel emotions through the very core of my being. And she knew this was to be attained not through spirit guides, but through higher consciousness, achieved through focused meditation.

And so for a while I continued attending the spiritualist church and the development circle. At the same time Gill was helping me to develop in other ways, broadening my knowledge and abilities – and showing me how to channel the psychic gift which seemed to have awakened in me and was becoming stronger. She was helping me to develop, control and harness it.

Three significant things happened during the course of the year, or so I attended the spiritualist church. The first, as I have described, was a sense of my own development, under Gill's guidance and, to a lesser extent, from my involvement with the spiritualist church itself. The second was an invite for John and I to attend a 'fledgling' evening at Newark Spiritualist Church in Nottinghamshire.

Perhaps the most significant of these things was the interpretation of my strongest vision to date, which was perhaps to have the biggest effect on my own sense of destiny and the kind of work I wanted to do.

Shortly before I had met Gill that first time I had experienced a very powerful vision. I struggled to understand what it meant. But I knew it was an awakening of a higher consciousness and a sign of the direction I should take – and how my own 'Gift' should be used. Again, Gill was there to help me fully understand what it meant – and give me the encouragement and support to follow my destiny as a psychic...

Chapter 9

As I sat in the front room, gazing from the window at the large Oak tree outside swaying in the keen summer breeze, my eyes began to focus on its many leaves. Suddenly, the green canopy seemed to be drawing me in as the leaves danced and trembled in the wind blowing through the branches. And then they all took on individual faces and became a mass of people, swaying from side to side; faces and hands all reaching out for my help. But how could I help them? Was this to be my destiny? Was each of the many thousands of leaves an individual person calling to me for guidance?

The vision faded as rapidly as it had come. It left me shaken and a little drained. And bewildered. There had been no warning. The day had been in no way unusual. Nothing remarkable had happened to trigger the experience, which seemed vivid and real. But it did give me the first sense of my own destiny. And there was no mistaking what I felt: That my calling would be to help people who needed the sort of guidance I might be able to provide. Yet I was barely 15 years old, struggling to find my place in the world and on the threshold of becoming an adult. It was Gill who was able to add meaning to the vision in the months ahead – and give me the tools to develop my abilities, which were as yet still emerging.

When I told her about the vision I had experienced she

expressed no surprise. It seemed clear to her. She confirmed my own feelings that I would be called upon to help many people as my psychic abilities developed. And she said she would help me. Like Granny Lizzie, I think Gill also had a strong sense of my destiny before I realised myself. And she helped me to develop, giving meaning to my psychic experiences, showing me how to channel, control and interpret what I was feeling.

They say all holy men experience a powerful vision to signal a higher state of spiritual awareness. I believe that the 'vision tree' I saw from my window that summer's day was the coming of my higher consciousness. Perhaps that was my awakening. I certainly remember it as a turning point, giving me my first sense that I had the 'Gift' to use for a purpose – and that it was to be applied in helping others; that I had a calling, even though I did not fully understand what it was, or how I would achieve it. Gill was to become my second mentor, following on from my Grandmother.

And I was in good hands. I think Granny Lizzie would have approved.

Now actively involved with the spiritualist church and its development circle, I remember John and I were asked to attend the Newark Spiritualist Church, which we accepted without any further thought, expecting the usual service we were already familiar with. But we were tricked! When we arrived the event turned out to be a 'fledgeling' evening at which we would be called upon to demonstrate our own abilities publicly for the first time as developing mediums.

Although we were assured we were ready to demonstrate our respective 'talents', I remember I felt sick to the stomach with nerves, as I realised we were to make a short appearance before the assembled audience from the platform. And though the 'audience' was very welcoming, when it came to my turn I remember breaking into a cold sweat, as all my worst fears came flooding back to haunt me. Could I really pull it off? Would I fail? Would I be rejected again?

As I was summoned onstage in my mind I called out to Granny Lizzie and asked her for strength and guidance. And then I felt she was there. As I was looking down at the people assembled below me, I noticed they were smiling warmly. Suddenly confidence flowed through me and I found myself beginning to speak, singling out a lady before me to relay the messages I was receiving. Images and voices came to me. I spoke again, in a voice which sounded alien to me. And she seemed able to relate to everything I told her. I focused on no more then four people in total. In each instance I seemed to be receiving messages and information about them which made absolute sense. And before I knew it, my ordeal was over and there was a round of applause. I could scarcely believe what I had just done.

Soon afterwards I was asked to conduct services in Loughborough and at spiritualist churches across the East Midlands on my own, which I did. And I began to develop a reputation as a gifted young medium. But as my abilities developed and my confidence grew, I began to realise that mediumship was not what I felt I wanted to deliver. My involvement had allowed me to build my faith and confidence in my own abilities, but there were too many limitations on what I was expected to do as a member of the spiritualist church.

I had recently taken up Raj Yoga to help with my visualisation and found meditation relaxing, fulfilling, putting me in touch with my higher consciousness. When I mentioned the sessions within the church I was reprimanded by the medium running the circle – and told I could not do both. I would have to choose. It was at that point I realised that the spiritualist church was not for me. I hold the freedom of thought and expression as very precious. Besides, you can't put limits on a Gypsy boy!

Gill was very open and supportive and told me I must follow my own path. She was always an encouraging inspiration. "Don't be dictated to by anyone, if it doesn't feel right," I can still hear her telling me. And that is how it felt. So I ended my involvement with the spiritualist church. I was barely 16 and had left school without any qualifications and no idea of what was to become of me. I had started my first manual job at a local textile factory, working long hours. But I kept in touch with Gill and shortly after distancing myself from the spiritualist church I attended a local psychic fair and watched how those taking part worked. Later I approached the organiser, told him about myself and asked if I could take part in the next one. He agreed to give me a try and an invitation was extended for me to attend my first psychic fair.

That was a new world for me, in which egos would clash, and showmanship and contacts were too often part of the success of the psychics who took part. And yet they seemed to make a living, even those whose talents were clearly dubious. I remember sitting at my table that first time feeling a little lost. Barely anyone came to see me, or showed any interest. But I learned. The key seemed to be to deliver a demonstration; to give a talk explaining how you worked and what you might see in your prospective clients. It was as simple as that. The next time I did exactly that. And people began to come to my table.

At first, it was hard going. I remember taking part in fairs all over the East Midlands, while working hard at the textile factory day in, day out. But gradually, over the course of the next six months, or so I began developing my own style and building up my own clientele. People began to want to see me for readings privately and slowly, but surely my experience and my reputation began to grow. And I was learning all the time.

When I started private readings I would ask for a personal trinket to hold from the person who sat before me, such as a ring, a necklace, or a wrist watch. I would use it to focus on and tune in, picking up the vibrations it gave off. And for a long time it worked well. But as the months and years passed, my psychic abilities have strengthened and I simply open up my chakras and let the images and thoughts that come run through me, interpreting them as I go along.

Sometimes spirits come to me and guide me. But usually I can see right into the person that comes to me even before they have taken their seat. I see them; know them intimately. And instinctively I seem able to tell them what they need to know, giving the best guidance I can. The rest is up to them.

Gill encouraged me all the way. Often in the early days of my career I would seek her advice on how to develop myself further, how to relax, protect myself. How to interpret better what I could see and feel. Even how to present myself. And if I ever held any doubts about myself, she was there. Though she passed away some years ago from cancer as a relatively young woman, I can hear her voice still, that final time I saw her, as she lay terminally ill in bed. She smiled warmly and said to me: "Always be yourself, my dear!" Soon afterwards the morphine kicked in and she sank into a peaceful sleep. It was the last thing she ever said to me before she died, a last goodbye.

"Always be yourself," she'd whispered. And I always have, always will.

Chapter 10

It begins with energising the body, clearing of the mind and the opening of the chakras, the body's centres of spiritual power. That's how I prepare to 'tune in' before a reading as I sit before a client. But that's only half the story. I was taught by Gill how to switch my energy centres on and off each morning before I begin my working day. And my ritual always begins first thing by taking my dog Bruno for a walk across the fields, rain, or shine. When I return to the house I reach out to my higher consciousness through what Roman Catholics might describe as prayer. I'll call it meditation. Silent, focused contemplation when I ask for the power of love and my guardian angels to guide me, and give me the strength to help my brothers and sisters. These will be the clients I will see during the day ahead, old and new.

Tuning in is quite a good way to describe 'switching on' and opening those energy centres, rather like tuning a TV set. It isn't so hard to imagine that there are unseen forces, or energies our minds can tap into. We already know there are invisible forces all around us we can measure and harness: TV, radio, mobile phone signals, for example. Even though we can't see them, they are there and can relay incredible amounts of information globally, invisibly, accessed by the touch of a button on the latest devices. It is just that there is no current measure of what the human mind can do, if trained, focused and tuned to the energy fields which naturally surround us. Imagine, for one moment the powers of the universe! It is already there for us to see all around us in nature and the changing of the seasons.

Next I begin to tap psychic energy by opening my crown chakra on top of the skull. Energy is important for work, and especially the kind of work I do. I have known too many psychics who have become drained and exhausted, giving up after only a few years. Burnt out. But the technique Gill taught me has kept me energised for many decades now. I visualise a flower opening on top of my head to awaken this chakra and I bring in three colours. First of all is green energy. I imagine filling my body with it, allowing it to drift down slowly like smoke, from the top of my head to the tips of my toes, filling me with light. Green is for the physical, relaxing muscles, slowing the heart rate and bringing the physical organs into harmony.

When it has filled my body, then I change my visualisation to blue. The blue merges into the green until I am fully immersed in this second colour. Blue is for the intellect, the mind, to relax and take away all negative thought. It puts me in 'neutral'. So when the physical and the mental are in harmony, just like tuning a musical instrument, I bring in the final colour. It is the colour of the sun. Some describe it as golden, or brilliant white light, to push away darkness, illuminating and joining with the universe. With mind and body in harmony and with the light within me to drive out doubt and fear, and all that comes with them, I feel ready. When filled, I then close down, rather like having taken breakfast, spiritually energised and ready for the day ahead.

My involvement with the Spiritualist Church as a young man was very much my apprenticeship. But like any artist, or writer, I began to develop my own style, my own development with

Gill's help, leaving any trappings behind that weren't part of that. I did not want to use tarot cards, or sand, or crystal balls that some people use as tools. Psychometry, the use of a small personal trinket from those I prepared to read to help me tune in, I also began to find unnecessary as time passed. My skills – and confidence – grew as I found everything I needed was within me.

And my style? I use humour to break the ice and help people relax. I guess I am very down to earth. There is no pretence; no show. Be they rich, or poor, successful, lost or lonely, every soul is treated with the same courtesy, respect and given the same warm welcome. Some say psychics and clairvoyants prey on the vulnerable. But that's not true. My clients come from all backgrounds, all racial groups, all ages. Mine include academics, doctors, police officers. Professional, highly educated people. These are not people easily impressed. They come from all walks of life. Some people who come to me are desperate for help. Others simply want guidance or advice and many of my clients are successful business people who base critical commercial decisions on what I tell them.

Those who come for the first time aren't always sure about this happy, cheerful person they have never met before or how to respond. But I have been this way for many years and generally, people warm to it and welcome the honest, earthy approach. When a client arrives I try to make them feel welcome.

I offer them a tea or coffee and invite them to sit down, either next to me or opposite.

Most will sit as far from me as they can! For first-time clients I try to explain as much as I can about what I do and how I do it. I try to take ignorance away and help them to understand that what I do is actually a very natural thing – and not something to be frightened of.

I suppose to many it must be strange and disconcerting to have someone they have never met before telling them about the most intimate details of their personal lives. And, because it defies current scientific explanation, many people come to test me and put up barriers. I must confess, I obtain the greatest job satisfaction from sceptics, leaving shocked, surprised, even amazed, trying to understand how I have been able to reveal so much about their lives, their hopes, their deepest fears... and their fondest dreams.

I close my eyes. And I open my third eye chakra. I visualise a flower opening slowly in the centre of my forehead, until its petals are extended and it is in full bloom. It's where we all visualise images if we close our eyes and think of something, right there, in the centre of our forehead. The technique of opening this chakra is like a trigger mechanism to tell the subconscious that it is in psychic mode, like switching channels on a TV.

Once it is open I focus on the solar plexus chakra, which lies just above the stomach, at the base of the breastbone. This is the emotional chakra, where people feel 'butterflies' at times of great sorrow, for example, in times of bereavement or ecstatic joy, such as being in love.

When both these chakras are open, I ask my third eye to look wherever I feel the client needs immediate help. It might be in the area of finance and work, or bereavement and loss, sometimes indecision, health issues, or relationship confusion. I see these things in symbols and feel emotions through the solar plexus chakra from the person in front of me.

In this sense I become that person; feel that person and portray them as an actor would. Once analysed, I ask the third eye to show me possible outcomes and the best decisions to be made at this time for the most favourable result. And then I have to put the images, the feelings, the emotion, sometimes even voices I hear, into words that people can understand.

It is a very responsible position to be put in, I am aware. And yet any of my own doubts in my abilities have proven to be unfounded over the years, so that now I trust totally what my higher consciousness tells me. Like playing an instrument, you need a degree of natural talent to start. Then it comes down to practice – and experience of life to add to a mature and compassionate reading.

Now I can describe people even at distance, or over the telephone across continents, picking up what they are like, even their physical attributes. Or by simply by being told a name to tune into. And that includes children, not only as they are now, but as they grow and mature. Many of my clients give testimony to my accuracy and provide feedback, which is valuable to me – and provides ongoing confirmation that what I see and feel is a true reflection of things past, present and even future in the course of my work. Sometimes clients contact me to share excitedly that something I predicted many months, even years ago, has come to pass.

Indeed, the world turns. Science too is advancing at pace. And with it our understanding of the world around us through that knowledge is rapidly expanding. As a species we are evolving, using more of our brains than ever before. This greater awareness is essentially within our logical mind. Still we use only a small fraction of our brains! But in the process of widening scientific knowledge we all too often neglect our primitive, instinctive, or you might say intuitive mind. And yet it is this primitive side that I am tapping into – a part increasingly sidelined like some distant memory as we come to rely more and more on technology. We are, if you like, becoming spiritually impoverished the more materially and technically minded we become. To fully appreciate the world around us, including ourselves, we have to embrace our spirituality – a higher consciousness and a harmony with the natural elements and forces that surround us if we are to find fulfilment, along with its self-healing potential. So what does the future hold for us? And is it set?

People often ask me about fate and destiny and whether or not I believe in it. In short, yes I do. That is not to say a person's destiny cannot be changed, perhaps as a result of a reading I may give, or something I have revealed to them, which makes them change course. And you might ask: How can that be destiny? It's changed. It is not set. I look at it this way.

If someone is drawn to see me, then you could argue that is part of their destiny. Just as if as the result of that visit the course of their lives has changed, perhaps that was fate. It was meant to happen. While I can see likely outcomes of a person's future, I also believe we each of us has choice of free will in all aspects of life. And you might argue further, a person's destiny might include a reading and a change in the course of their lives as a result. But at the end of the day, whether clients take the advice I offer is entirely their decision. While you might lead a horse to water, as they say, you cannot make it drink. Therefore, if you are drawn to see me, it may be part of your destiny. But whether you choose to use the information that has been revealed, remains very much up to you!

Of course, sometimes my timing on future outcomes has been

out. But my feelings, my visions and the readings I give have tended to be very accurate, up to 90 per cent and more, I have been told. That's borne out by the feedback from clients, some of whom have come back time and time again, even becoming friends. And that's made me feel I have a real purpose in life. That this beautiful gift gives me hope, strength and the ability to help many people before my time is spent. That is what I believe the 'vision tree' that came to me as I gazed from the window that summer's day meant. It's all about love and compassion and dispelling fear. It has been said the only thing to fear is fear itself. I subscribe to that. So often it is our own fears that hold us back from reaching our potential and achieving our dreams...

Chapter 11

My own future did not seem clear to me. At the time of Gill's death I was still realising my psychic potential and things were far from straightforward. Gill's passing had shaken me. In the three years or so I knew her she was always kind, supportive and highly positive. She taught me the techniques which I still use today. She was more than a friend. She showed me the way. That was the precious gift she gave to me in the relatively short time we had together. But now she was gone.

When she died I was working at the textile factory in Loughborough. At the same time I was attending psychic fairs all over the East Midlands to build my experience, my clientele and my reputation. I would have been 17, or 18 and still living at home. And there was a lot going on at the time, good and bad. Tensions seemed to be growing between my parents. But like most young people of my age I was out in the evenings socialising when I could, drinking and dancing. It was a vibrant scene in Loughborough, which at that time still retained its manufacturing industry. People had work in the town and money in their pockets. And, after the working week they wanted to have a good time.

Increasingly I felt less like going home, or that I wanted to be there. Perhaps it is the same with all young adults. But the home atmosphere was not good and I think all of us felt it. My father was in decline. His drinking was finally catching up with him and his health was beginning to fail. But he was working. He'd taken a job as a labourer at Brush Engineering, where I also ended up working. But any spare cash my father earned, he squandered at the pub. By this time we had moved to a slightly larger council house in Queens Road, where I still had my own room. I found myself with a job at the Brush purely by accident. Or was it fate! I was standing outside the factory site one afternoon to meet a friend. Lee was late finishing and suddenly, as I stood there waiting for him, the manager popped his head out of the gate to see if a candidate for a job interview had shown up.

"You've not come for the job then?"

"No," I replied, adding I was waiting for my friend.

"Do you want a job?" he asked me. I thought about it for a moment and I decided to find out more.

That's how easy it was in the 1970s and 1980s to get a job, before our manufacturing industries went into terminal decline!

Brush Engineering offered more money than I was making in my job at the textile factory, better conditions... and there was overtime. Lots of it. So I took the work. And it proved to be a good move. I worked long hours and managed to save. I was also starting to earn some additional cash from the psychic fairs I was attending all over the East Midlands and the private readings that were flowing from them, even though they were irregular and sporadic. Often I would conduct readings in a back room at the local pub. It wasn't ideal, but for a while there was no alternative.

But things at home were not pleasant and I realised I needed my own place. My mum and dad's relationship was growing ever more distant and there were frequent arguments. My father's time outside work was dominated by his social life at the local pub, the Greyhound on Nottingham Road, or the Gate, neither of which exist today, where he would play dominoes, drinking himself stupid, chain smoking which seemed accepted as a normal part of leisure time.

My mother would stay at home, still cleaning and preparing meals as she always had, waiting for him to return home, often the worse for wear. And so the distance between them widened further. Sad to think how they once were, so very deeply in love when first they had met and married.

I was the first of their children to move out, at the relatively young age of 20. I had been working all hours, putting as much money aside as I could to secure a mortgage on my first property, a small terraced house in the town for the princely sum of £17,000. This was a different kind of freedom and allowed me the sort of independence and privacy I had never before experienced. So although my working hours were long and hard, I felt I had achieved something. And for a while life seemed to progress at a breakneck pace, working at the Brush during the day, giving private readings in the evenings, often still spending weekends at psychic fairs. Somehow I even managed to fit in a social life a couple of evenings a week.

It can't have been very long after getting my own place that I remember visiting my parents one day. And my father said the most profound thing I ever remember him expressing.

He was not an emotional man. Or spiritual. I don't know where my mother was, perhaps in the kitchen, but as he came downstairs our gaze met and he looked me straight in the eye. He said he wouldn't be here much longer and asked me to look after my mother. I was taken aback. I knew immediately what he meant. He felt he was not long for this world. In some ways he may not have been a very good husband, but I do believe he loved my mother until the end, even though he struggled to show it.

Within the next year my father was diagnosed with lung cancer. I remember it was a harsh winter of 1983 and, following the diagnosis, his health went into rapid decline. The bitterly cold weather continued into the new year and before the advent of spring he appeared to be the shadow of himself. Then one day at work, a phone call came for me at Brush in the middle of the afternoon. It was from Loughborough Hospital and I was to come right away. My dad didn't have much time left. I remember, I actually dropped the phone.

When I arrived at the hospital, still in my blue overalls, my mother, brother and sisters, along with cousins, aunts and uncles were already gathered around the bed in which my father lay, his face covered by an oxygen mask, from which he took ever more shallow breaths. He was barely conscious. Though it was still winter, inside the hospital it was stiflingly hot. After a while he asked my mother to make sure we went across the road to get something to eat and we all trooped out to head for the nearby chippy. It was a relief to be out in the cool air. While we were queueing outside my father took his final breath. When we returned he had gone. I think he felt the end was near; that he had not wanted us to see him die and had effectively sent us away. After a short and bitter battle he had left this world at the age of 56.

I remember standing over his bed feeling totally emotionally numb. Around me my brother and sisters, and my mother were crying, distraught in their grief. But I wasn't feeling anything, except an overwhelming and sudden sense of responsibility for those around me.

A cousin, observing my lack of emotion commented. "Why aren't you upset?"

"Because he is not suffering any more; he's at peace," I remember replying quite calmly.

And it was true. I felt a sense of relief that he was at rest.

But I also felt a sense of responsibility for those around me; that I had to be strong. Perhaps it was because I was the eldest son. That's how it felt. And I am still coming to terms with my deferred emotions today. Perhaps I can identify more with my father now that I am myself older.

But did I ever really know him? He displayed little emotion in all the years I knew him. Perhaps he was simply not able to. So who was Joseph Deadman? What were his deepest thoughts and his fondest dreams? I am not sure I will ever know. To be free to roam from place to place, that's for sure, which is how I like to imagine him now. But I can only guess how much the loss of that lifestyle he had known for so many years led to his drinking or was part of the tragedy that unfolded for him as life and love slipped away from him. It must have been hard for him.

Strangely, I feel it is only now that I am fully able to grieve for him, coming to terms with that loss. Perhaps because I did not allow myself to grieve at the time. Or perhaps it is because I too am approaching the same age at which his own life ended. In any case, I do not judge him, or think of him unkindly. He was my father and I loved him, even though he was unable to show love in return... and he is a part of who I am.

Chapter 12

As I gazed towards leaden skies, with the raw chill of the winter's day against my face, it was hard to know how to feel. I shivered, wrapped my scarf a little tighter against the cold and tried to shrug off any thoughts of sadness, before heading across town on foot to the house in Queens Road. The sudden passing of my father had affected us all in different ways.

I was still numb, not really feeling anything, except a strong sense of responsibility for my immediate family. Even though I now had my own place and work – and was still practising Karate – I would pass my mother's house on the way home from the Brush and drop in to make sure she was all right. But I needn't have worried. For her the show had to go on. And before I left she would always force-feed me a hot meal while I was there, whether I wanted it or not!

She was a very nurturing woman. In all the years she cared for us as children we never went hungry, even though sometimes there was little money. And after my father's death she continued to shop every day, keeping the house clean, caring for my bother and two sisters, and carrying on as normal. So if she was grief-stricken, she never showed it. She was a very hard and determined woman, for whom my three siblings still at home were very much the centre of her life. She also had her faith and remained a devout Roman Catholic to the end, never questioning the 'slings and arrows of outrageous fortune'

; her way. I never heard her complain once. Nor did
sh........ly express grief, or sadness, or sorrow in the days
following her loss.

And my siblings? My sister Sabina, 18 months my junior, was
always very enterprising and hard-working. She had a job at
the local Berni Inns steak house as a waitress and would work
long hours. I think it helped her. Like me, she had a certain
detachment from my father. And it is true he had his favourites,
which were my younger sister Lilian, the baby of the family and
especially my brother Joe, who was without doubt closest to my
father, the apple of his eye.

Sabina seemed to cope reasonably well, perhaps because
like me, she was older and already working, with a degree of
independence. And life did go on. I remember I was courting
my first girlfriend and wanted to impress her by going for a
steak meal with all the trimmings at the Berni.

Not being very confident with the opposite sex, unlike my
friends, I was quite shy with girls in the romantic sense.

We had just ordered our steaks and waited in the reception area
with a drink for our names to be called over the tannoy system
when the meal was ready. When it came to our turn, whose
voice should come loud and clear over the speakers, but my
sister's, who announced gleefully that the table for two for *Mr
Deadhead* was ready! Much to my embarrassment, everyone
stared as *Mr Deadhead* rose to take what seemed a very long
walk to the table in the dining area with my girlfriend, my face
as red as a beetroot! Bless her, Sabina had a wicked sense
of mischief, as we all had and was never afraid to poke fun
at her elder brother. In fact all of us retain a keen sense of
humour in the situations which present themselves in everyday
experience, can mimic accents, and revel in making fun of

ourselves and others.

My sister is also very psychic, although she has never been interested in developing her 'Gift'. But she reminded me of a story recently from her childhood, when she might have been 11 or 12 years old. At the time there were many derelict and abandoned properties in the town, either waiting for demolition, or refurbishment. And often as children we would explore and hunt out different objects, left in forgotten corners. Anything from jars of pickles to discarded fire extinguishers, even old helmets, or gas masks from the last war. And sometimes we would pretend to be soldiers, using whatever abandoned items we could find and our imaginations could put to use in our war games.

My sister holds a lifelong fascination for gardens and beautiful flowers. She tells a story of one day walking alone down an entry at the side of one such abandoned property to find herself standing at a gate. Peeping over the top she could see a beautiful rear garden beyond it, filled with wonderful flowers of all the colours of the rainbow. And there, standing in the garden was an old lady, smiling at her, who asked her what she was doing there.

"Coming to look at your beautiful garden," my sister replied. "Can I come back again?"

"Yes, of course you can, my dear," the elderly woman smiled in answer. "Come back tomorrow."

And with that my sister excitedly hurried away to tell her friends.

The next day Sabina returned with several girls to show them the beautiful garden, as the woman had suggested. She led them through the passage at the side of the abandoned house.

As they emerged to view the back garden, they came to the gate, which was open and their gaze fell upon a neglected, overgrown garden full of weeds. The experience of the beautiful garden and the disappointment on her return is still vivid in Sabina's mind. I believe she initially saw a vision of the garden as it once had been and the lady who had lived in the house many years previously.

My brother Joe was closest to my Dad, with similar interests and personalities. He was definitely my father's favourite. He taught him to drive well before me and Joe accompanied him on most of his trips. The effect of my father's sudden decline and death was profound. Being younger and more reliant on his parents, especially my father, he reacted to the bereavement with anger. Soon he was making friends with those regarded as 'tough guys', regularly getting into fights, sometimes resulting in a night in the cells. But even then, there was no escaping a wholesome Sunday lunch from my mother and I remember her asking me to take a roast dinner to the police station so that Joe could eat it in his cell!

Then my brother started to come home with tattoos, which, looking back, was I think a rebellion against everything he had known. Neither my father, or I have tattoos. I remember Dad always saying they were something *Gorgias* had. Besides, they were seen as a potential form of identification if you had trouble with the law; something that might limit you and therefore not something Romanies were keen on. The stress on my mother must have been considerable, as he spiralled out of control and he would increasingly return home drunk, just as my father had in his day. Sadly, through time, the excesses took their toll and Joe has struggled with a life-long dependency on alcohol.

Lilian my youngest sister is the baby of the family and was still at school at that time. Yet she had a good network of friends, which helped support her. She always confided in me, as the big brother she looked up to, as she still does to this day. She tells me she likes to see me as I remind her of my Dad, having inherited his physical features. But in fact, I was close to both my sisters.

So I took them under my wing and we would go out dancing together, me being the big brother accompanying them for a night out in the town and we shared some good memories of that period. All of us have a natural sense of rhythm and are good dancers. At that time there was a wonderful community spirit in Loughborough – and everyone seemed to know each other. There was seldom any trouble.

Lilian's talents came out in later life as a therapist in alternative health techniques, practising reiki, crystal healing and aromatherapy, as she does today. She is, in fact, a very powerful healer, with a heightened sense of spiritual awareness. And although my father passed away when she was 16, or 17, she seems to have coped well. Yet Joe seemed to reject all efforts to help him. It was as if there was no filling the void in his life left by my father. I did try to keep an eye on all my siblings, despite a very hectic work schedule, including increasing bookings for private readings. And so life continued...

Work was getting busier and busier. And with the rising demand for my psychic readings my confidence grew during this period, which helped divert me from the passing of my father. In addition I had all the responsibilities that came with adult life: A mortgage, bills to be paid and work to be done. But with it came a refreshing sense of independence and self-reliance.

One day I was working near Burton Upon Trent and stopped off afterwards on the way home, just short of Ashby-de-la-Zouch. The Mother Hubbard Country Pub, set back from the road looked inviting and I wanted to recover and unwind. So I slowed, swinging the motorbike I now rode into the courtyard and glided to a gentle halt. I took off my helmet and gloves and strode inside. The landlady greeted me with a warm smile and as I ordered a drink I noticed she was heavily pregnant. A strong image presented itself to me and, as sometimes happens spontaneously I had to say something. "Twin boys," I exclaimed as casually as I could.

Her name was Charley, who returned my gaze with a look of surprise and asked me how I knew, having just found out herself. So I told her what I did, that I was a clairvoyant and she asked with concern if the children would be okay. I told her that they would be fine, but would come two weeks early.

Then we chatted about this and that before she was drawn away to serve other customers. But I gave her my business card before I left.

"There'll be fine, I promise you," I repeated cheerfully. "But they will be early!"

And I stepped out into the courtyard as the sun began to set.

Some weeks later the phone rang and it was Charley. She wanted to thank me. She and her baby boys were well. But they had come two weeks early. She had taken my advice which had allowed her prepare for their premature arrival. Her husband Graham was so impressed with what I had predicted that he contacted the Burton Mail, who came to interview me, resulting in a substantial article in the local paper. Even better, I was invited to the pub once a week when people would come to see me for readings which I gave in the back room. An unexpected encounter with Charley and a few simple words of advice had led to additional work, my first newspaper exposure and expanding my reputation. Things were looking up...

Leap of faith

Chapter 13

It happens when you least expect it. But I guess that is life and the surprises, both good and bad it springs upon us without warning. Even for me! I had a house of my own, plenty of work and a growing reputation as a psychic, which is where I felt my calling lay. I had something of a social life too. I'd had a couple of girlfriends, but nothing serious. And although quite shy romantically with women, I felt relatively good about myself. Still in my early twenties, I felt there was something missing, though. I wanted someone to love and accept me for who I was. I suppose I wanted someone to share my life with and start a family. And I felt ready.

Strange how these things happen. I was walking from the corner shop in Queens Road, where I had just picked up some milk and bread for my mother when I paused to glance along the street... and there she was. The young lady cycling towards me on the racing bike had long flowing hair and the most beautiful smile I think I had ever seen. I remember she seemed confident, elegant and attractive in her polo neck sweater, jeans and high brown boots.

As she approached our eyes met and I instinctively smiled back at her, and felt a racing in my heart. It was one of those moments in life. There was something about her. Something unusual. Something different. Certainly she was attractive, but it was as though I had been struck by a thunderbolt and as she disappeared into the distance, I felt it was an opportunity lost. Should have said something, Deadman! Yet I'd been rooted to the spot! I had no idea who she was. What I did know was that I wanted to see her again. But the moment was gone. The only consolation was that she must surely be living locally. And perhaps she'd pass by again.

In the immediate days that followed I thought about the girl on the racing cycle a great deal. But inevitably life goes on and as time passed, she slipped from my consciousness. Besides, I was still working hard. And I had no reason to think I might see her again anytime soon. Then one evening I nipped down to the local pub my dad frequented, a good venue for local bands, who often played rock music.

The place was also gaining a reputation as a bikers' pub and occasionally I would pull in and have a beer. On this particular evening I thought I'd check out the local band.

When I approached the bar there were already a few familiar faces to be seen, including Mick, a friend of mine, and he introduced me to some people he was with. They included a young lady who was lodging in the shared house he was living in. Her name was Kate. And she was none other than the young woman I had seen on the pushbike in Queens Road. We just grinned stupidly at each other, as she recognised me in the same instant and then she unleashed that beautiful smile of hers. After talking to her for a while she revealed she too had a motorbike and my interest in her grew further. She struck me as incredibly feminine, yet tomboyish too. It seemed an irresistible combination to me.

She went on to become a regular at the venues we both liked to attend and as our friendship grew I asked her if she would be my girlfriend. Fully expecting a refusal, I was surprised when without hesitation she said she would. I was ecstatic, totally smitten and like a fool in love. The weeks that followed seemed dreamlike, unreal, as we began to spend more and more time together. After courting for some months, even going on motorcycle and camping trips together, we became closer than ever. So I plucked up the courage to ask her to marry me.

At first she looked shocked and frightened. And she turned me down. A feeling of rejection and foolishness filled me. But still, I told myself I would be patient and hoped that she would change her mind. So we continued to see each other. And our feelings seemed to deepen, so that sometime later I asked her again if we could marry – and this time she said 'yes'! It was one of the happiest days of my life. Now planning our future, living together became a topic of conversation. This was the stuff of dreams and all I had ever wanted now seemed possible: A partner to share my life with and raise a family. My time had come...

Kate was a beautiful woman, with long auburn hair and dreamy blue eyes. And that winning smile! Her father had served in the second world war and had later risen to a senior post in the civil service before retiring. I always felt as though I should salute whenever I met him!

I suppose her background was upper middle class. Sadly Kate had lost her mother in infancy, something which I feel affected her deeply in later life. But at this time we couldn't have been happier. I felt fortune was smiling on us.

Work at the Brush was steady and my reputation as a psychic was beginning to take off. And I had found the woman of my dreams. What more could anyone ask for?

The wedding took place in the village church at East Leake, set within the rolling countryside on the Nottinghamshire and Leicestershire border, a stone's throw from Loughborough. My mother was not overly thrilled with the Church of England venue, because of her own Roman Catholic faith, but accepted it. Yet it was a strange gathering of two very different families that day. Kate's comparatively wealthy relatives mixing with my more earthy Romany family. Yet somehow we pulled it off without major incident!

We had decided to put my house on the market. Kate had inherited money from her Aunty Joan, who had been like a second mother to her. And she now had her own three-bedroom property in Loughborough, which is where we had decided to start our married life – and in fact ended up staying there for the next year or two. But now we were talking about starting a family and we discussed the prospect of buying a larger house between us. At that time properties were still affordable for ordinary working people, not at today's over-inflated 'silly' prices.

And we looked to the countryside. With my Romany Gypsy background I yearned to be near fields and close to nature. Kate said she knew of a small country pub called The Star and, both being keen cyclists at the time, we headed out to the village of West Leake on our pushbikes one Summer's afternoon, about six miles outside Loughborough. After a drink or two we walked into the village to stretch our legs. Around us lay beautiful, lush countryside as we strolled along the country lane hand-in-hand, passed the small wooded coppice towards the the first of the houses we could see ahead of us.

As we entered the village where the road takes a sharp bend, and a sign signals the beginning of West Leake we saw a striking detached property set back from the road, positioned within a large garden. And it was displaying a 'For Sale' board. Both of us fell in love with the house at first sight. When we contacted the estate agent we learned it was on the market for £87,000, was set within a quarter of an acre and came with an option to buy six acres of pasture land directly opposite.

This was a massive leap forward for two people who had respectively owned properties under £20,000. When we saw the bank manager, he took a sharp intake of breath. Mr Davis, I remember as quite fatherly. At the time I was earning good money and had always paid my mortgage on time. Kate was working at the nearby East Midlands Airport for Orion Air as a bilingual secretary, being gifted in French, Italian and German. Mr Davis took another deep breath. But, our joint incomes were sufficient for the required mortgage, which he agreed, adding his advice that we surely knew the consequences if we did not keep up the payments. And we shook hands.

Our offer for the house and the six acres of land went into the estate agent and was accepted. I can't describe that incredible rush of joy and expectation I felt for the future and sharing the life in prospect with the woman I adored at my side. Things could surely not be better. I had found a woman I loved, possessed my dream house and was a landowner. It wasn't long before I had a caravan standing in the field opposite and horse of my own, a magnificent 16.2 ex steeplechaser, adding joy upon joy...

Chapter 14

I woke up one morning and suddenly I knew. This was going to be the day! My work was going from strength to strength, a mixture of private readings, attending psychic fairs the length and breadth of the country and holding down a job at the Brush. In fact, I had too much work. Overtime at the works was plentiful, regular and expected to help meet contract deadlines. But it was exhausting, given the energy I was also putting into my psychic work.

But now I no longer held any doubts about my future direction: The 'Gift' bestowed upon me was to be used to help and guide people, and I was bound to follow that destiny. There were no half measures. To be successful I would be required to pour all my belief, my hopes, my dreams, my energy into helping others through the abilities I held. The feeling of self-belief was overwhelming. It would have to be. So I had made up my mind. Kate was worried about financial security seeing as we were now planning to start a family. And that was perhaps understandable. Yet my future seemed clear to me.

I took a deep breath, knocked on the foreman's office door and stepped in.

"What can I do for you, Deadman?" he asked. "I want to hand in my notice," I replied without any hesitation.

His reaction was one of total shock and he looked at me as if suddenly confronted by a complete madman. Did I know what I was doing? Did I have another job?

When I told him I would be working for myself it only seemed to confirm his view that I had lost my mind. He reminded me I was lucky to have a job at Brush Engineering. And he had a point.

The plant was a major employer in the region, offering above average wages and many additional benefits to its workers.

I explained to him that what he thought was my hobby would become my livelihood and that I was taking up my psychic work on a full-time basis. And I remember, he laughed out loud, told me I was a fool and that I would never have a job that paid so well ever again. But I told him I had thought things through and would not be changing my mind. And I left the office with the foreman still shaking his head.

My workmates expressed similar views while I worked my notice, telling me on a daily basis during my final week with them that I was being foolish. But there was no going back. I was more certain than ever and felt my required 'leap of faith' would be rewarded with success.

Finally that last day arrived. I left the works site for the very last time, stepping from the gate beyond the barbed wired walls patrolled by security guards to 'freedom'. Some people enjoy the security of established routines and strict working protocols. But for me it had at times seemed like a prison. The Gypsy in me was too strong to be restrained, or suppressed. And by this time I had confidence in myself and my work. There was the sense of excitement and of adventure – a control over my own destiny – was overpowering and left me with no feelings of doubt about the big step I had taken. I suppose most Gypsy people strive to be reliant on themselves and need a feeling of freedom without conventional limits. And that feeling was deep within me too.

Shortly afterwards one of my clients, who had been visiting from the States, asked if I would come to Houston, Texas. She had been deeply impressed by the reading I gave for her and wanted to write an article for the *Indigo Sun*, a magazine widely distributed across Texas, all the way down to Mexican border. The article was published and she sent it in the post, along with a renewed invitation to visit Texas, all expenses paid. It seemed the opportunity of a lifetime, which I accepted.

It was quite an experience: The heat, the landscape, the people. The sheer scale of everything and sense of space. Everyone made me feel very welcome and seemed fascinated, not just by the work I did, but also by my English background. They loved my accent and kept asking me to repeat the phrase 'Me duck', the term of endearment common across Leicestershire and Nottinghamshire. And I was in demand, conducting many private readings and improving my links with the US, which I still maintain, along with many clients I remain in touch with today. I had a fantastic time. Everything I could possibly wish for seemed to coming true!

It was around this time that I received a call from the local newspaper.

The journalist on the line said he had heard about the work I do and my success, and asked if he could come to interview me. A few days later the young reporter arrived with a photographer. His name was Andy and as we talked we seemed to hit it off immediately. We were similar ages, although I remember he was a good few inches taller, with striking black hair. I could feel his enquiring personality, a genuine interest and open mindedness, which proved to be the basis, as things turned out, of a life-long friendship. That man was Andy Goss.

I knew then he was going places. I sensed he would travel, to the States... to South Asia and Africa, even before Andy ever considered which way his career might be going. In the event, he began to progress within print journalism. And it wasn't long before I heard from him again. He was working on the daily newspaper in Northampton and wanted to run a further article about me and my work. The exposure led to interest across the Northamptonshire area, which helped during those early days following my decision to focus on my work full-time. And we kept in touch, an association which led to a collaboration of several articles in which we would investigate a series of hauntings across the East Midlands for the newspaper.

During this fruitful time Kate and I decided to try for our first child, conceiving my son, James. As soon as we discovered Kate was pregnant we both knew it would be a boy and called him 'little Jimmy' as he as developing in the womb. Shortly into the pregnancy, Kate handed in her notice at East Midlands Airport to tend our beautiful garden in West Leake, in which she spent many hours daily, right up until the labour pains began one late Winter's afternoon in 1990.

Kate wasn't sure it was the real thing and thought the pains would subside, so she rested for a while. But as the pains became stronger and more frequent it became apparent the baby was on its way. Driving to the Nottingham City Hospital I prayed it would not be a difficult birth. Thankfully there were no complications and within a matter of hours my first son James was born. Any father witnessing the birth of his child will know that rush of relief and joy at seeing a little human being brought into the world. And thank God mother and baby were well. With tears of joy rolling down my cheeks I held my little boy for the first time. Now I was a father, only too happy to take up the the responsibility of the new life I held in my hands.

My mother had always been very maternal and expressive in her love, something sadly my father had found difficult to display. Love. It is as important to an infant as the milk from a mother's breast. It is the language all children instinctively understand and need to feel through smiles and hugs and care. It is probably the purest form of love that exists, as close to unconditional love as we will ever come. The love for a child. If children receive such love from birth it provides a strong foundation and in turn allows them to express themselves in later life, providing emotional strength to face those triumphs and disasters in their own journeys as they grow to become adults.

So I had become a daddy, and with it came a sense of happiness and fulfillment I had never known before. At my side, the woman I loved, the mother of my son, living in the house of our dreams. In addition I was becoming increasingly successful in my work which provided an income which had exceeded my initial expectations. Ironically I bumped into my old foreman from the Brush one day in Loughborough town centre a year or two after I had left. I asked Colin how the lads were – and he admitted to me sheepishly they had all been made redundant a while back. He was not laughing any more! The belief in myself had paid off, thank God and I have never looked back...

Chapter 15

A thin mist hung above the graveyard like a pale spectre in the darkness as we made our way silently through the tombstones towards the ancient chapel. It was a bitter, moonless night in October. In my hand the huge iron key we had collected from the old manor house, cold against my skin. My companion kept his flash light towards the ground so that we could follow the narrow pathway which led towards the oak door which would allow us access to the final resting place of Sir Robert Bannister. All around me I could see the lights of many spirits which hovered above the graveyard. I was thankful the journalist beside me remained blissfully unaware of them as we made our way slowly towards the stone chapel coming into view through the darkness.

The small south Northamptonshire village of Passenham was known for its hauntings. And the imposing medieval manor house and its small church was said to be the centre of things.

Lying on the banks of the winding Great Ouse as the river meanders through the gentle Northamptonshire countryside the village now seems a forgotten backwater in county's history. And yet some 400 years ago it was a different story.

The tale they still like to tell is of Bannister, the wicked landowner who added to the manor house in the early Stewart period, overseeing the surrounding land with an iron hand and extracting hefty taxes from his poor tenant farmers they could barely afford to pay. He's even credited with ruthlessly pulling down the village, leaving only the church and a few farmhouses standing so that his property might escape the new Poor Rates introduced by the Crown to support the most impoverished families on the estate. Some say it was simply to improve his view across the fields from the leaded windows on the upper floors of his newly expanded country retreat. You might guess he was both dreaded and despised.

It was therefore with no great sadness that villagers learned of his sudden and untimely end. Sir Robert had gone hunting one afternoon, as was his pleasure. And as his horse unexpectedly spooked and reared, the hapless Bannister was thrown from his steed, breaking his neck in the awkward fall, while his foot remained lodged within the stirrup of his saddle. Yet it is said even as Bannister fell from his horse he shrieked "Steady, steady, I'm not ready" in a bid to cheat death. The hapless horse galloped at pace across the fields before clattering up to the manor steps, dragging Bannister's mangled body behind it, his head barely still attached to its torso.

They said as they laid him to rest in the chapel within the manor grounds that the wind rose and a ghostly voice was heard echoing the last words he had uttered as he had fallen from his horse. And so it was arranged that the marble slab which was to cover his tomb was of exceptional weight and thickness. Just to make sure it kept him where he was finally laid to rest. Yet local legend has it that on those stormy winter's nights when the wind is wild and the moon is high the clattering of a phantom horse with the headless spectre of Bannister can still be seen galloping across the fields to the very gates of the ancient manor house...

So here we were, approaching the tomb of Passenham's headless horseman in a bid to discover whether Bannister's spirit truly still lingered four centuries on, or whether the story could finally be laid to rest. As we stood outside the chapel on that dark and misty night I looked at Andy, the Northampton journalist with me to document our ghost hunting adventure and we both took a deep breath. I slid the large key into the lock and turned it until I heard a satisfying clunk which reverberated through the silence of the cool evening air. The studded oak door slowly swung open and Andy directed the beam from his torch into the the darkness within. And suddenly we both gave a start.

The beam fell directly upon the face of Sir Robert Bannister... immortalised in a marble bust just inside the chapel entrance.

"Found him!" Andy exclaimed. And we both glanced at each other and smiled nervously. Then we stepped inside, our footsteps echoing on the ancient flagstones as we approached that very marble slab said to prevent Bannister from ever rising again. There was a mustiness in the air. But I could feel nothing. Nothing unusual. And certainly no sign of the evil Sir Robert Bannister. Andy was watching me as I closed my eyes and tried to pick up anything from Bannister that might remain. But there was nothing. No evil spirit. "He's long gone," I told him.

"And actually, I don't pick up anything bad about the man. At least nothing unusual for the times, which were brutal. Nothing, mate," I added. I wasn't sure if Andy's look was one of relief or disappointment.

"Sorry mate," I repeated.

"You're sure."

"Yeah, I'm sure," I assured him.

For a moment we both stood there in the semi darkness.

"It's back to the manor then," Andy said with a sense of resignation. "Let's take up the offer of tea and biscuits."

The manor's current owner had been wonderfully welcoming and accommodating. We had picked up the church key from him a little earlier, when he had offered us a hot drink. And yet the evening was to take a further twist when we returned with the key and to take up his very kind offer before leaving Passenham.

"No sign of our horseman then," said our host at the manor with a smile.

"None," I replied.

"I'm sorry you've had a wasted evening," he added, then paused, before adding: "There's something else you might like to see..." And he gestured for us to follow him. He led us outside and pointed to the magnificent tithe barn across the courtyard.

"I have something I would like to show you." And we followed him as he strode off across the courtyard towards the thatched barn.

He pulled the door open and we gazed into the darkness with expectation while he fumbled for the light switch. As he flipped the switch the naked bulbs suddenly glared brightly to reveal row upon row of classic cars under the lights. We were awe-struck. Our host explained he was an auctioneer by by trade, but collected the classic vehicles as a hobby. Andy and I stared at each other. But our host seemed in his element. He pointed out a classic limousine with sweeping wings and white walled tyres, dating from the 1940s. "Isn't she a beauty?"

As we stood before the majestic classic car I was immediately overcome by images associated with the vehicle. In my mind I saw two lovers on the back seat, locked in a passionate embrace. The man seemed older, distinguished and the woman was beautiful. I felt she was a famous young actress but that the affair they were engaged in was secret, even scandalous. When I told our host he was himself amazed. The car had once belonged to the Italian movie director Roberto Rossellini who had an illicit affair with Hollywood star Ingrid Bergman, which caused a sensation in America in 1950. Both were married at the time and the scandal almost finished the career of the Swedish actress.

I was directed to another vehicle, an Army jeep in immaculate condition. There wasn't a scratch on it. Yet I felt it had seen action in the last world war, in Africa and had been severely damaged. I saw shells exploding all around. I sensed men had been killed as it was hit by shellfire. Again, the man was incredulous. The vehicle had sustained serious damage in Africa, but had since been shipped over and fully restored. And so the evening continued as I seemed able to reveal the history associated with each vehicle I stood before.

And yet there was more. The barn itself was 400 years old and had its own history. A rush of images flowed into my mind... of battle-weary, bloodied soldiers with swords and muskets resting... injured men being tended. The barn had been used by Civil War troops as a field hospital for the wounded. But I also knew the structure had been used for more sinister purposes and I saw bodies hanging from the beams overhead. Scores of men had been executed here. I could see them hanging lifelessly.

Looking for restless spirits

Our host said he was not aware, although he believed several battles had been fought in the area and Cromwell's men were said to have camped in the village in the days leading up to the decisive Battle of Naseby to the north of the county. I told him I was certain the troops had been in the barn and that there was still equipment under the compacted mud floor, if ever he cared to excavate, including weapons and armour. And so ended what turned out to be a memorable evening, even though Sir Robert Bannister, the object of our visit had long since passed on.

We left our host promising one day to return and hoped to persuade him to start digging to reveal the treasures I sensed were still hidden within the barn. But we never did and for all I know it is still there waiting to be discovered. It was one of a series of adventures Andy and I embarked on in the months ahead, investigating haunted pubs, theatres and country homes, where I was able to sense passed events and whether lingering spirits were real or imagined. We certainly have a few tales to tell... and yes, I did encounter a number of restless spirits. Some have moved on, while others continue to make their presence known.

And my journalist friend Andy? He never got to see the apparition he hoped to. Or perhaps he did and remains blissfully unaware. 'Ghosts' make their presence known in many ways, come in many shapes and forms. We live our lives among the dead. Spirits of those who have gone, but have not been able to pass on to the next world are all around us in our everyday lives. The boundaries between the living and the dead are sometimes very thin. And sometimes it is about being in the right place at the right time. We just need to open our minds to allow ourselves to see and feel and sense... and some are able to do it more naturally than others...

Chapter 16

The sergeant barked the order and, assault rifle in hand, I threw myself onto the ground, breathing heavily as I lay prostrate on my stomach. Beneath me I could feel the hard earth which the long grass in which I lay failed to cushion. And I was sweating profusely under the weight of full army kit, rasping for air from the physical exertion of moving rapidly cross country to out-manoeuvre an imaginary enemy force. As I raised the weapon, squinting along its barrel for potential targets, as I had been trained, it began to rain. A long, damp night under the stars was in prospect. But I was loving it, out in the open countryside. I took comfort knowing there were 10 or 12 guys almost invisible in their camouflage around me, on whom I could rely and who were facing the same physical hardship.

With so much psychic work, which is mentally and emotionally exhausting, I needed something to help me switch off. Something to distract mind and body. And always being relatively physically fit, with a love of the outdoors, this seemed ideal. I had joined the Army reserve force, enlisting with 203 Squadron (logistics), based in Loughborough and had become a part-time soldier! The training was hard, being pushed mentally and physically to extreme limits, in all situations, from sub-zero, to tropical conditions. And I thrived on it. It wasn't that I wanted to fight, or kill people. Rather it was an idea that I was proud of my country and prepared to defend it and everything it stood for. That naturally included my loved ones, if it came to it.

I had always held a fascination for World War One and World War Two history. Even as a boy. And with my father in the scrap iron business, I'd often pick up souvenirs. I remember one time going with my Dad to the Bernard Morris scrapyard in the town, where there was an abundance of old military vehicles, some even dating back to the last war. One day I climbed into an old rusting tank and searched the various storage lockers. I couldn't believe my luck as I pulled one of them open to discover a German helmet that had been hidden there for years, which I still have to this day. It sparked my interest in collecting militaria.

I must admit, I liked the idea of experiencing the military for real. It seemed to make sense to experience and see life through the eyes of a soldier.

Now I was in the Army, be it as a part-time member of the Territorials. And I was enjoying every minute. Everyone made me feel welcome. The comradeship and the loyalty to each other is something all those who have served will recognise. You took care of each other. Watched each other's backs.

There was a code and you needed to know you could rely on your buddies in life, or death scenarios. I suppose there was also a nurturing protective side to it. You would support your comrades in all situations. That came naturally to me. The other aspect I liked was that it did not matter what your background was. Once you were in uniform, you were on the same team, through thick and thin. And of course, I revelled in the outdoor exercises.

It also represented fulfilling a dream. Quite literally. Since I had been a boy of 14 I had experienced the same recurring dream for many years, that I was driving a big Heavy Goods Vehicle, pulling a trailer behind me. This was one of the skills I gained with 203 Squadron, obtaining my HGV licence. Suddenly the dream was broken as I became a driver for the Army, moving supplies and weapons, sometimes to front line troops. The dream had always featured trucks that were left-hand drive, which had puzzled me. When I came to drive some of the heavy vehicles for the Army, they were in fact left-hand drive, explaining the dream many years later.

Kate was very supportive of the time I spent away. This was mainly at weekends, but occasionally involved longer trips. I think she knew how much it helped me to switch off from my psychic work. She accepted I would sometimes be on exercise for short periods and encouraged me to spend as much time as I wanted pursuing my new hobby. Certainly I have good memories of my years with 203 Squadron and was able to travel to places like Canada and the Ascension Islands, seeing and experiencing things I never would have in civilian life. And it was the perfect distraction from my psychic work which continued to keep me busy!

Kate had developed her own reflexology skills and was practising from home, bringing in additional income while still caring for our little boy. Her therapy was complimentary to my own work and in every way we seemed a perfect team.

Family life couldn't be better and fulfilled all my expectations of what life should be. During this time my wife conceived our beautiful daughter, Katharine. It was a happy time. The pregnancy was without complications and when the time came I even cut the cord, and was the first to cuddle and embrace my darling baby girl. It made me feel I had a special bond with my daughter, which I still feel today.

A little girl and my boy. Perfect. At the time both Kate and I felt one of each was plenty. We both seemed fulfilled with our lives. The jigsaw was complete. But as they say, if things seem too good to be true they probably are! Perhaps I was too happy to see. I was deeply in love. I now had two beautiful children I adored. Materially we had everything we needed and my work was plentiful and satisfying. In addition, my involvement in the Army was an added bonus, and had brought me new friends and experience which I enjoyed. Yet I loved being at home with my young family best of all.

Looking back that period does now seem idyllic. A dream. But it seemed real to me.

I guess I didn't notice that Kate was slowly becoming more distant. Perhaps I was too consumed by happiness to see. She never really spoke about her own deeper feelings, or any problems and always seemed to have a smile on her face. That beautiful smile. So I assumed she was as happy as I was. They say love is blind and maybe that is true. While everything seemed wonderful on the surface, things were not entirely as they appeared to be.

Increasingly, Kate seemed to need long periods on her own. Often she would go for long walks in the countryside by herself. She said she needed time away from the children and enjoyed being with nature to contemplate. And I would look after the kids until she returned, sometimes hours later. Yet it seemed to do her good. She appeared refreshed and relaxed when she returned. It didn't seem too much to ask, or unnatural. The strain of two young children was taking it out of her. And I was only too happy to share the load, which came natural to me. Besides, I loved being with the children. So I didn't feel there was anything seriously wrong. Family life, with all its demands, still seemed sweet. Everything had been wonderful. Yet the biggest test was about to come...

A period of darkness

Chapter 17

It was like a hammer blow. I hadn't seen it coming. Kate said she was leaving me. When she told me she didn't think she had ever truly loved me it was like a knife to the heart. My whole world seemed to collapse in an instant. At first I couldn't really take it in. The very foundations of my life were crumbling, threatening to topple everything around me I had built over the last few years; everything I believed in. It was my worst nightmare. And I remember staring at her in disbelief, struggling to understand the enormity of what she was saying.

Looking back now I think the unhappiness built within Kate over time. She wasn't able to express her unhappiness and I think the loss of her own mother in infancy was a big factor. As I have mentioned, I think the need to love and nurture children is the most precious gift we can give them – and is vitally important for them to draw on in later life. I don't feel Kate had this and I think it led to her restlessness, her sense of personal confusion as an adult.

The little she told me about her innermost thoughts stemmed from the loss of her mother when she was little and her father being left with two daughters to care for. He was a rigid man, quite Victorian in outlook and very judgemental, who was unable to express his emotions. What I gathered myself and what Kate confirmed was that she never felt loved by her father. The closest she came to being loved came from her father's sister, her Aunty Joan before she passed away, and whom I met and remember as a warm and giving lady. Certainly she was someone whom Kate could confide in and when she died Kate, who was by then in her early twenties had no-one to go to.

As she struggled with her inner turmoil, Kate's need for more time to herself became more desperate until one day she must have felt she simply couldn't go on. She told me she wanted her 'freedom'. She said I was a good husband and a father. She didn't blame me in any way. But she said she felt the children would be better off with me. She didn't want the house; it was the children's home. But she said she needed money, so that she could have her own house where the kids could visit and maintain contact. As you might imagine, the shock I felt was totally overwhelming. I initially struggled to absorb what she was saying.

Naturally, I suggested we could work things out. And I believed it. I loved her and was ready to support her in every way I could. But no matter how much I begged and pleaded with her, assuring her she was loved and needed, she wouldn't change her mind. My daughter Katharine was barely four years old and her brother James was seven. They needed her too. But she was adamant. She had to go. And for the first time I began to wonder if I had ever really known her at all.

And what to tell the children. They were still so young. Having always been close to them in every way, I wasn't sure how I could explain that Mummy was leaving them. What was I to say? I hadn't yet processed the enormity of what seemed to be happening myself. Suddenly the skies were dark and I could no longer feel the warmth of the sun I had bathed in upon me any more. Now my life as I had known it was disintegrating. I seemed under attack from all sides. And still people wanted to see me and my work was keeping me busier than ever at a desperately sad time in my own life.

To raise the money Kate had asked for I sold the land I held opposite the house, along with the horse and caravan, which only added to the loss of everything I held precious and had worked so hard for. The land sold, the divorce in progress, after receiving her money Kate packed her bags and she was gone from my life. A dark void of despair was upon me, of acute bereavement and loss. My heart was broken and the woman I loved did not love me. My own confidence hit rock bottom and those old feelings of rejection I had known as a little Gypsy boy came back to haunt me with a vengeance.

People have often said to me: You're a psychic. Surely you must have seen it coming. But when it comes to my own life, I am psychically blind. It just doesn't work for me and I am not sure why. Perhaps the personal emotion is a barrier, clouding my vision. Or perhaps we are not meant to see our own destiny. Maybe, if I knew what was coming I would be tempted to stay in bed some days! I suppose it begs the question why I should look into the lives of other people, their passed, present... and future. Isn't that a contradiction? It might be, if I was to reveal everything I saw, or was shown.

But I believe I only see what is helpful to guide the person who comes to me. Yes, there are sometimes warnings. I am able to give people advice. But only if destiny dictates that the information should be shared. I believe we are destined to make certain journeys, have certain experiences, good and bad. It is these which will shape the people we become. And some experiences bring valuable life lessons which need to be learned. Not everyone learns, of course. And sometimes more lessons are needed. But I believe every experience can be good, has its purpose, if we can draw knowledge from it and become better people.

My children, Katharine and James

During this terrible period of separation help came from unexpected sources. It is a strange thing that in the very darkest times, some of those friends you feel you might rely on are suddenly not there. And support comes from the most unanticipated quarters. Someone you barely know does something truly wonderful.

Kate had been more than a wife to me. I considered her a friend and a partner in every way. And she had helped with my work, organising client appointments, keeping my diary up to date, paying the bills, which had been an additional support. Especially as I suffer from dyslexia and even struggle to put a set of numbers down in the right order. Now suddenly I was on my own, a single parent with a business to run. I had to keep up with the demands of caring for two small children, who were missing their mother, cooking, cleaning feeding... doing what two parents normally do while still trying to earn a living. And for a while I couldn't seem to function. I am ashamed to say I fell behind with getting back to clients and in arranging appointments for readings, bills went unpaid. I couldn't seem to keep up with things and for the very first time in my life I fell into debt.

I must have been close to despair. Emotionally exhausted I seemed barely able to cope. I was fighting a daily battle against depression, I now realise. And for the first time in my life I felt anger, particularly when I learned my wife had started to see another man. How could she do this to me? More importantly, how could she do it to the children. Why had she simply given up on us? Was life so terribly unbearable? Clearly it was for her. And that is very sad. It had seemed beautiful and fulfilling to me. I felt Kate had thrown away the chance of life-long happiness with both hands. I know she felt she had no other choice. So a period of darkness and despair overtook me as I wrestled to come to terms with what had happened. I couldn't see a clear way forward. My debts were rising and by this time I was already three months behind on the mortgage. Repossession of the house in West Leake seemed a real prospect. Yet in the midst of this desolate, desperate period somebody came to help in my hour of need when I least of all expected it. At that time I seemed in free fall. Simply put, things seemed to be going from bad to worse. There was no light on the horizon until a new lady came into my life who must be mentioned. She showed me genuine friendship and kindness at a time I most needed them...

Chapter 18

I had, like many evenings, fallen exhausted into a restless sleep when the dream came. It was a dark night and I was outdoors, cold and alone. The drizzle was relentless against my naked skin and I was vulnerable in every way, with nothing to protect me. In this dark and dismal dream there was no comfort. And I could hear wolves howling in the distance, slowly drawing closer. I could hear them coming my way. They had picked up my scent and were out to destroy me.

I began to run headlong though the darkness and into a forest. Up ahead through the trees I could make out a dim light and felt I had to reach it somehow, while the wolves were steadily gaining on me at my heels, wanting to devour me. The evils of this world, the wolves, were demons trying to destroy me at a vulnerable time with no-one to protect me. And still I was running, trying to reach the light, which was a place of safety. As I came closer I could make out the glow was coming from a church, whose door was open.

Panting and rasping for breath I finally reached the church and entered the doorway, slamming it shut just as the wolves were upon me. Leaning against it I was close to exhaustion, gasping for air. I could hear the wolves outside, scraping and clawing at the door. But they couldn't get in...

Suddenly I woke in a cold sweat. It was always the same

recurring dream during this very dark period in my life. I wasn't sure what it meant at the time, but I knew it wasn't good. It seemed I was in a battle for my very survival.

Looking back I think the wolves in my dream were my fears and doubts, the weaknesses that could have destroyed me, not individually, but as a pack. The running was my desperation to escape them, running blindly. And the church, a symbol of sanctuary and peace, an oasis in the darkness all around me where my fears were unable to enter and where I knew I would finally be safe.

I have come to realise that my faith in the power of love and in positive energy was my true sanctuary, allowing me to overcome all the fears that were besetting me. But for now I was still facing a sea of troubles, battling to keep myself afloat with no hope on the horizon I could see. When help came it was from an unlikely source I could not have imagined.

Many of my clients have seen me regularly over many years. And some of them have become friends. Elaine was one such client. Based in Falmouth, on the Cornish south coast I didn't see her often, but we went back a few years and she had always kept in touch. When she introduced me to a friend of hers who was living in the East Midlands, little could I have known what a profound effect this person would have in helping me through the difficult times I faced.

Her name was Sarah. She was a single parent herself, bringing up three sons on her own over the years. She had heard about my situation through Elaine and offered to help me with my admin, getting back to clients, organising bookings for readings, even helping to juggle my finances. And she became a good friend, coming over two, or three times a week. She even signposted me to benefits I could claim as a single parent, including working tax credit, which I hadn't even heard about before.

It is no exaggeration to say that Sarah saved my house and took a great burden from my soul and mind. She showed genuine love and kindness in a way that was utterly unselfish. And she became my girlfriend. She told me she could see the goodness in me and she could feel my pain. She was also extremely generous and took me on holidays to Italy and the Czech Republic, lifting me from despair and making me feel human again. Over the months her feelings for me deepened and she told me she had fallen in love with me.

Sadly I was still in great emotional pain and I was far from ready for a long-term commitment, still holding strong feelings for my ex-wife. To this day I regret I could not return Sarah's love. I think I was still struggling to overcome depression and the only love I seemed able to give was for my children. She told me she wanted us to live together and although I knew she would be a wonderful partner whose love for me was strong and sincere, I wasn't ready. I needed more time. I was simply in no condition to return it the love she gave to me.

And so the relationship with Sarah ended. I said I would like to remain friends, but she told me she was unable to only be a friend. Her feelings were too strong. And so this wonderful lady left my life. I do not like to hurt anyone, but I know I hurt Sarah very much.

It wasn't intentional, but was a result of my circumstances. Yet I still carry the guilt for hurting someone I know was very special. I believe she played a major part in bringing me back from the very brink.

Many years have now passed, but I have held her in my prayers every day. It was a long time before I saw her again, when both Sarah and I happened to attend our mutual friend Elaine's sixtieth birthday party in Falmouth. It was my chance to apologise for the pain I caused her. She had since married and was there with her husband, who seemed a really nice guy. When I talked to her she told me she had suffered greatly at the time, but she forgave me, lifting a great weight from my shoulders. I will always be grateful to her.

Back then, as I still struggled to come to terms as a single parent, life had to go on. I had to change and adapt. Above all, I had to be strong for the children. But I was in better financial shape thanks to Sarah. And she had played a big part in giving me hope, not least of all through her own love and kindness. And I still had my business, though it became more home-based. All my nurturing skills went into overdrive. Sometimes, I am sure I overcompensated, over-feeding the children. I even pressed their school uniforms and polished their shoes daily. I think they must have been the best-dressed kids in school! But I was rising to the challenge of life without a partner and being both mother and father to my young children.

My own personal grief was secondary. Every night I would smile, snuggle with the kids and read bedtime stories, laughing and having fun with them. I never showed my tears to them. Nor did I ever criticise their absent mother. It was only when they had gone to bed and were fast asleep that the darkest moments came and loneliness seemed to fall like a heavy, smothering blanket of despair. They were sometimes the longest nights.

Yet somehow I carried on, juggling being a single parent with making a living. Of course, I had to finish with 203 Squadron. My Army days were over. Similarly, any plans for overseas work were also shelved, although I am still in touch with clients in the States. I had to adapt. And the primary focus had to be the children, who needed their Daddy more than ever.

And they needed him at home.

And the years passed. The children grew and began to develop into young people, with their own personalities. My son, James was starting to bring friends home and so was Katharine. There were suddenly sleepovers and parties with tents in the garden. I have always been quite relaxed about things and have a genuine fondness for children. The more the merrier. And that may well stem back to my Gypsy roots, as it is very much in the Romany culture. And everybody seemed to want to come. And before I knew it I seemed to have become something of a pied piper! But I was simply pleased to provide a happy home environment and to see my own children having fun.

For many years my psychic work has been primarily home-based. The ambitious plans I may have once held to travel with my 'Gift' overseas to build up a significant clientele in the US and perhaps Canada, or across Europe were not possible while my children have been growing up. They have been my priority. And that's as it should be.

But I was able to change the way in which I worked. At first it never occurred to me that I might be able to give as good a reading by phone as if I had the person sitting right there before me. I had never tried. It was another client based in Evesham who was unable to travel to see me who suggested it. So we tried. I suppose there was no reason to think I couldn't. After all, I had been tuning into family and friends of clients at distance for years. And sure enough, the reading went beautifully well. Holding the phone in my hand I could see the images and feel the emotion just as powerfully and accurately as if the lady had been sitting in the same room beside me.

It transformed the way I worked, particularly when the children were still young. It also meant I could build and maintain a clientele overseas, which I have.

I am not saying that life has been easy over the last 20 years since my wife left me. Loneliness has often been my only companion on many a long evening when the children were tucked up in bed. Any single parent will know that fatigue is all too often a familiar friend. But somehow you cope. The love for your children drives you on to unbelievable limits of endurance. And faith. Faith that someday the sun will shine again and that the love will win through.

That is sometimes all we have, yet in some ways it is everything.

Looking back at those difficult years after the marriage ended and the loss of so much I held precious I now know I passed the biggest test I ever faced. The stakes were high. It might easily have destroyed me. But I feel I gained strength, confidence and wisdom in overcoming my worst fears – and winning through. I think too it has made me a better person; a better psychic. I believe that when we overcome our worst fears, those greatest losses, then fear no longer holds any power over us... and that liberates our souls and makes us better human beings.

So perhaps there is a truism in those oft quoted words: The only thing we have to fear is fear itself.

Certainly fear can be the greatest obstacle in achieving our hopes, our dreams, our destiny. But with the light of faith, of hope and love the darkness will not prevail. It will be driven out, not just from me, but from all of us...

Love, life and the universe

Chapter 19

People often ask me: What's it all about? This journey called life! I could answer in three words: Faith; hope; charity. In a sense they represent everything we should carry with us along the way. Most will associate them with Christianity, but they are central themes to all the major religions. With good reason. They are big pointers in mapping the way and finding fulfilment. Certainly love and light helped steer me through the darkest of times. And faith. A belief that despite the hardships we face, love will win through, if we remain steadfast in our determination to believe in the power of good, that all things pass and to be kind to others, even in our own deepest sorrows.

This is the torch we must carry through the most testing times to hold our path and drive back the darkness. And good will prevail, just as surely as the earth turns. I try to remind people with troubled lives that the sun always shines above the clouds, even though they might not be able to see it. Those clouds will pass, allowing them to be illuminated by the sunshine once more. But we must be strong in our belief. And sometimes we will falter. Sometimes we will lose our way.

Victory over the negative forces which impact our lives may sometimes come at great personal cost, often with acute emotional pain, even permanent loss. In my experience these trials will test us, often pushing us to the very limits of endurance. But they teach us about ourselves. Lessons need to be learned. It is how we develop into better human beings. And it is through our own suffering that we come to fully understand the suffering of others and are capable of feeling their pain, as well as our own. That's empathy, compassion, love.

Therefore the journeys we are all embarked on in this world can be seen as taking the good out of the bad – and learning. Learning to survive. Learning to be strong. Learning to love ourselves and others. I know about suffering, because I have suffered. It allows me to feel what others feel and to have empathy with their pain. At the end of the day, love is everything; the most potent force in the universe. Without it we are without soul; we are nothing, because ultimately we come into this world with nothing and we leave with nothing. Except the love and enlightenment we gain throughout our lives. I believe we take that with us. I have faith.

But what is faith? To me faith centres on love, peace and tolerance.

And if asked about my own religious belief, even though I was brought up Roman Catholic, I might reply, as Gandhi did: "I am a Muslim a Hindu a Christian and a Jew..." I might add Buddhism and others too. Don't we all share the same basic dreams and desires, have the same fundamental needs? And surely the key themes of all the major religions centre on peace and love. It's the same message. The very idea that religions should divide us is a perverse contradiction. Faith, whatever it may be, should surely unite us in our common aims for good. Sadly, faiths are all too easily corrupted and manipulated by men. And greed.

As for material wealth? What is that without a sense of joy and fulfilment? It is hollow and empty.

And can we, should we be comfortable if we have more than we need and others go hungry, have their lives cut short by preventable disease, or sleep out in the cold? Should we really rest easy in our beds knowing others are suffering when we often have so much more than we actually need? In some ways these are deep philosophical questions. In another sense, it is very simple.

We must rise above our own desires and the temptation to acquire more and more material wealth. Because it comes at the expense our spiritual health, which requires nurturing through acts of kindness and compassion to those less fortunate, who are often disadvantaged simply by accident of birth, or circumstance.

As Jesus said: "It is easier for a camel to pass through the eye of a needle than for a rich man to enter the kingdom of God." You can't take it with you! Regardless of personal faith, whoever Jesus was, he must have been great philosopher and visionary.

But charity does begin at home, as the oft-quoted saying goes. So be kind to yourself too. Learn to know and love yourself. It is about self-awareness, which is a fundamental on the journey to truly love others, as you would yourself. Yet where does one begin...?

I believe my own calling is to put smiles on faces and bring light to push back the darkness. My joy and satisfaction comes from guiding someone through dark times. It makes me feel I have a purpose; to help others find their way. It is why I have often described myself as a psychic counsellor. I don't do what I do for financial gain. I earn enough to live and retain my independence. That independence is important to me. It means I am free from conventional restrictions and able to work in the way I feel I need to, which may not be to everyone's taste.

But it is very liberating to have this ability and know from feedback how accurately I am able to 'see' and 'feel' the things which shape other people's lives. And how I have helped those who come to see me.

Of course, I use my third eye chakra every day and as such, it comes entirely naturally to me. It may allow me to see something in somebody's life at the most unexpected moments... even on holiday, in a pub, at a football match. But if I can help someone, I will. That comes with the territory, as they say. It makes me feel I was destined to meet that person at that particular time to help them – and that a higher force works through me to place me in the right place at the right moment. Equally, I can switch off completely if I have to – and sometimes need to.

The gift I have is both a blessing and a curse, as you might imagine. Seeing the suffering and the trauma in people's lives is not always easy. Often I actually feel it too. And it can be mentally and emotionally very draining.

Yet I also seem able to tap into energy from the universe to recharge the batteries, so to speak. As I have said previously, I take steps every day to meditate, to relax and to draw on the positive energy all around us. And occasionally, usually when I need it the most, I will feel a rush of positive energy fill me. I literally feel supercharged. For no particular reason, at no particular time. Nor am I conscious of calling in power on those occasions. It just seems to happen. The last time I felt this incredible surge of energy I had just returned home one evening from a well-received demonstration of my 'Gift' locally. Although exhausted as I stood ready to raid the fridge for something to eat I suddenly I felt positive, glowing energy fill me from head to toe where I stood – and the kitchen light exploded, fusing the whole downstairs circuit!

But we can all tap the positive forces around us. We simply have to open our hearts and minds to the beauty that surrounds us. We need to take a step back. By the same token, we should be aware of what is less good. Certainly 'living is easy with eyes closed, misunderstanding all you see...' The Beatles said it. What a great line. Open your eyes. The world is being seduced. Greed is the latest addiction. It's not a new problem, but mass media and an increasing reliance on technology is taking us away from spiritual contemplation and awareness like never before. We are becoming increasingly vulnerable to that seduction by those who wish to control us. And that is about power. It is about greed. It is about capitalism, fuelled by ever increasing consumer spending.

Again, there is nothing new about those in power trying to control the masses. What is frightening is the methods used harnessed with the powerful technology we have available at our fingertips. Ask yourself: Where do you obtain your information on which you base your judgements, your decisions, your life? Increasingly I fear we are becoming reliant on mass media: TV, radio, internet, social media... touching, shaping and influencing every aspect of our lives. The space for individual, contemplative thought is shrinking fast. So who controls these powerful platforms with so much influence over every aspect of our lives?

It's a sobering thought that everything you read, see, or hear is shaped by someone else's opinion or motive. Think about it. I am under no illusions that society, the media and governments employ armies of 'spin doctors'. These people know our psychology and how to manipulate and entrap people. It is no different really to the early days of empire, enticing people with glass beads for gold, water, or land rights, eventually stripping them of their independence. Make no mistake, it's all carefully orchestrated!

These people know our weaknesses and will target our lower intellect which embraces three main areas: Greed, gossip and sex. Pick up any popular newspaper and I guarantee you will find all three aspects covered extensively! And look at the rise of so-called reality TV programmes flourishing like never before, with vast audiences. People airing their personal problems in public for our amusement, often shouting like children as they lay bare their grievances and vices. Even their suffering. Are we not entertained? By people's misfortune, afflictions, people's pain? Is it really any different from watching gladiators in the arena, or lions tearing early Christians to shreds? Perhaps we are thankful that today it is not us. But in the words of the song made popular by the Manic Street Preachers, 'If you tolerate this your children will be next...'

Indeed, the real concern must be for our children. Many have forgotten how to play... how to interact with others and enjoy simple pleasures. But what example are we setting? We are isolating ourselves. Almost everyone seems in their own virtual world, plugged into games, or social media. Social? Far from it. How then, in this apparently advancing, sophisticated and socially aware world we have created, is it that more loneliness and mental health issues exist than ever before? It's reaching epidemic proportions. The social fabric of our society is breaking down. I believe it is because we are turning our backs on our need for spiritual fulfilment.

Yet that need can be met through the simplest social interactions. Spending time with family and friends, taking in the calming beauty of nature, or taking joy from the arts. All good for the soul.

But consumerism is the new God. People seem to want to escape the real world. Part of that escape is to buy something to feel good. And it does. For a very short time before the novelty wears off and something else needs to be bought. It is an obsession. Yet that need to buy and possess something new, something better seems insatiable. It becomes like an illness, an addiction. Because it doesn't really connect at a deeper, spiritual level. It's all superficial, fuelled by the society in which we live and those who control it. Consumerism. Sadly, the effect of this materialism is to suppress the things that bring us true fulfilment. It's destroying our very soul, eating away like a cancerous disease. The next time you decide to go and buy something, ask yourself, do I really need it?

Personally, I take great joy in experiencing the seasons, enjoying the countryside, watching beautiful sunsets and sunrises, feeling the sun upon me, or a breeze against my cheek, listening to the sound of the birds all around and taking in the power and the beauty of nature. It connects with a basic, primeval need to be close to and in harmony with the earth. And it costs nothing. Nor does it drain the world of its valuable resources. Instead of taking, shouldn't we focus on giving something back? Giving. Now there's a word. In my view, one never gives without receiving. Buddhists say the effects of a single smile has a ripple effect that can reverberate like a chain reaction across the universe... and eventually it will find its way back to you. That's karma. And that *is* something to feel good about.

Chapter 20

So you want to know about love, life and the universe? Here's my take, if you're sitting comfortably. Let me start at the beginning. If we accept life as a journey to be undertaken with experiences made along the way to shape our consciousness, our personalities, perhaps we should consider what we are. Scientists tell us we are largely made of water and carbon. And a few other elements. They also maintain we are highly evolved, sophisticated animals. How we ended up in this particular combination of elements, chemicals and electrical impulses is still a matter for debate. But animals nevertheless. Chimpanzees, our closest animal 'relative' share 99 per cent of our DNA! Yet there is one major difference which sets us apart. Our imagination. The ability to create images in our mind. To dream. To rise above our basic instincts. Some might also say the ability to feel, to love. Furthermore, we can communicate our images and ideas to each other. With that comes a desire to express the emotions we feel.

Whatever the difference is, it has allowed us to translate the images in our heads and put our ideas into practice, creating a range of tools and accessories giving us the edge and allowing us to climb to the top of the tree. At least on this particular rock in the universe! Look at the things we have achieved in a relatively short time. If the earth's history was represented by 24 hours, humans have been around for just one second!

That may be 200,000 years since homo-sapiens, as we know them evolved, but is only a tiny fraction of the 4.54 billion years since the earth was created.

Unfortunately man's wisdom seems to walk hand-in hand with his idiocy. We have harnessed unimaginable power by splitting the atom, put a man on the moon, not to mention innovations in technology that are commonplace across the developed world, like TV, motorcars and, almost unthinkable 30 years ago, the World Wide Web. Sadly our ingenuity to benefit mankind has also been equalled by our investment in killing each other more effectively – and on an industrial scale. And our ability and appetite to wage war seems undiminished over the millennia. Our basic instincts may easily be hidden, but beneath the surface we are as primitive as ever.

In fact we may even have regressed. Knowledge and wisdom has been lost. The world seems to be facing its worsed crisis for many centuries, losing its way.

Yet there is one other key difference that sets us apart from other animals.

Our need for spirituality, a sense of our place and purpose which has been apparent since the dawn of time as we know it and is evidenced in the earliest known civilisations. But, as mentioned in the previous chapter I believe opportunities afforded by incredible advances in technology are being misused and squandered. We are so impressed by our own cleverness it seems to me and an arrogance which may well be our undoing as we bask in the light of colossal achievement, our shadows taller than our souls. And that's the problem. We are neglecting our spiritual side, worshipping at the altar of materialism. A false idol in every sense. It is a backward step. Bad for society and bad for our spiritual wellbeing. And we are back to greed.

Every man for himself. Survival of the fittest. We might as well be back in our caves!

Fortunately, help and hope is at hand. We are gifted with great visionaries and spiritual leaders who reach out to us and show the way. In recent history one might list extraordinary people like Mahatma Gandhi, Martin Luther King, John Lennon... and yet I would struggle to name one today, even though the need for spiritual enlightenment is perhaps greater now than it has been for many decades. Who will be the next? You? I? The very quest for knowledge, enlightenment and freedom of thought is the first step... and no power on earth can stop it.

Mahatma Gandhi chose to live simply, touring almost naked, wearing little more than a loin cloth, barefooted, carrying a stick. He changed the course of history for millions, effectively ending one of the most powerful empires the world had ever seen, by peaceful means, without firing a single shot. Martin Luther-King, whose courageous visionary speeches still send shivers down my spine gave his life to establish meaningful freedom for black Americans. And John Lennon influenced millions by championing love and peace for all the world at the height of his fame. Prophets preaching love and brotherhood between people of all races and all faiths. All of them were assassinated. But they and their thoughts live on if we remember them, as we must.

There is a desperate need for great minds and souls, great leaders. But we should take heart. Just look around you at the good that exists in those helping others. We are not alone, neither in our fellow human beings, or indeed those with an extraordinary sense of enlightenment.

I believe in angels. They are all around us. They might be exist in the caring nurse, the cultivating teacher, the compassionate charity worker... or your friendly grocer down the road. In other words, they are people who set an example of love, kindness and sharing.

I believe angels walk among us on this earth and that they also exist as spiritual beings. I know I have been visited by such beautiful beings. Often when I need them the most. Sometimes they will visit us in our dreams. But it might be anywhere, anytime. You'll sense it. An overwhelming feeling of being loved. Waves and waves of unconditional love flowing through your mind, body and soul, reminding us we are never alone. An angel might even be a loved one, long departed but still watching over us.

Angels are those who have reached the highest levels of enlightenment and are not seduced by the darker forces and temptations that exist. They are incorruptible. Have you ever thought why angels are portrayed with haloes? An angel's halo symbolises a full circle of knowledge and wisdom directly above the crown chakra, which draws in universal power and energy... the forces of good. Angels are representatives of a higher force who take joy in the joy of others. They have passed all the tests of this world.

It is what we should all strive to become. Sometimes it might take several lifetimes. So yes, I do believe in reincarnation and that many of us have lived before. We return again and again learning new lessons to take us to that state of enlightenment. And some will take longer than others. More lifetimes. More suffering until we reach that state of peace, joy and enlightenment.

But we have free will and we can make our choices. And I will come back to love. The more love you radiate and invest, the more you will inherit. There may be times when you feel bitter and angry. When you feel resentful, even vengeful. But remember, two wrongs will not make a right. And once resentments take root, it is easy to lose the joy of life. It is as the old proverb goes, there is good and bad in all of us, like two wolves, constantly fighting within us. Which one will win out? The one you feed the most. Think about it. The choice really is ours. Take what good you can from the bad things which all of us will encounter in life. And learn the lessons. Turn them to positives.

If you ever want to contemplate our place in the universe, spend some time laying on your back, gazing up at the clouds on a summer's day as they lazily drift by. Look up at the stars in the night sky and consider the thousands of galaxies we now know exist. Or simply take a few moments to meditate each day in absolute silence on how to be the best person you possibly can. How can you be kinder, more compassionate? And you can begin to consider the incredible beauty of love, life and the universe and all its possibilities. And you won't ever be far from the right path... that's about what really matters. Spiritual fulfilment.

Chapter 21

What's it like to be Patrick Deadman? People seem to want to know. How does it feel to see and experience what I do as a psychic. In a word: Enlightening. Also draining. Painful. Fulfilling. It is uplifting, bringing joy to others and helping them along on life's journey to the best of my ability. That is how I feel the 'Gift' I have been given should be used. It is a responsibility. It is sometimes a burden. Imagine you suddenly feel what the person in front of you is experiencing in their personal life. You sense what is to come; what is in store for them. That kind of knowledge can be hard to bear. And sometimes I seek solitude, taking in the beauty and the energy of nature with Bruno, my faithful Jack Russell. Or sometimes in my own company. In the words of the famous actress Greta Garbo, there are times when "I want to be alone." Sometimes I simply need to switch off, away from the madding crowd.

But perhaps all of us should take that time out, especially in this seemingly ever more stressful, fast-moving world. Protecting mind, body and soul to keep ourselves in balance. We need to take a breather and step back from the hustle and bustle of an increasingly busy world, which bombards our senses like never before. I am seeing more and more stress in the clients that come to me, desperate for a sense of peace and harmony, free from ever spiralling financial, mental and emotional demands, trying to find purpose and direction while being driven along by a frantic pace of life. Step out of the whirlwind. Take refuge. And start to protect yourself. That's my advice for a longer, more fulfilled life.

Meditation is a good place to start. Learn to free your mind from worry, from the everyday stresses and strains of life. Some like to listen to peaceful music, or chanting. Myself, I enjoy the silence... absolute silence from the bustle of modern life, which relentlessly clutters our thoughts. Sometimes I'll slide in a disc, turn the volume up and blow off steam dancing around the kitchen to the raw exuberance of those early rock n' rollers. Or I will head for the countryside to seek solace in nature, resting my eyes on fields of green, or perhaps gaze up at the sky, watching the clouds drift by, revelling in the wonder of creation. Hearing the birds sing, or the sigh of a gentle breeze blowing are not distractions to me, but allow me to connect with the power, beauty and peace of nature. Try to be at one with yourself, the universe and all life around you.

Easier said than done. Perhaps. But learning to switch of and allow the mind to take a rest from the hustle and bustle around us is important for overall health. Stress these days is a killer. And if you don't allow your mind to find peace it will affect the body and materialise in physical effects. Our thoughts, feelings, beliefs, and attitudes can all positively or negatively affect our biological functioning. In other words, what we think and feel can affect how healthy we are! Medical science increasingly acknowledges, for example, the impact of poor mental health on the physical body, raising blood pressure, putting increased strain on the heart, lowering the body's defences and so on.

Diet too is important. Eating healthily and regularly to provide our bodies with the vitamins and the nutrients needed. You'd be surprised by just how much eating habits have changed over the last 50 years – and not for the better. Everything is available in the developed world. Just visit your local supermarket. Seasonal fruit and vegetables? Everything we could want is now there for us year-round and 24/7! Take for example your Christmas turkey, once an annual festive feast. Those turkeys are available every day now, if you wish. And treats. These are no longer occasional, but daily. Look at the amount of sweets and sugars we consume... at every opportunity.

A few words on the fast food epidemic. What a terrible indictment of the way we live our lives today that these outlets are practically on every street corner. Burgers and fries, fried chicken and fries. Everything with fries! But at least they provide a little lettuce to make us feel better. Look at the levels of obesity in the Western world, reaching epidemic proportions. Similarly our children are addicted to sugars at alarming levels. Ask any dentist about the the frequency and advance of dental decay in children now. Fillings and even teeth extractions before the age of 10 are becoming commonplace. And we've all heard the phrase 'comfort eating'. Comfort from what? The poor quality of life we are choosing to lead when we have more opportunities, more comforts at our fingertips than at any time in our history. What's that all about?

So food's important. And not just any 'junk' food to fill a hole. There's a lot to be said for good old-fashioned home cooking with fresh ingredients. And, of course, you know exactly what you are eating when you prepare the food yourself.

Not to mention the therapeutic benefits of creating your own dish, switching off from all else, giving your mind a breather. And it's creative! But again, it is about taking the time. And that seems to be in very short supply these days. Time. What a precious thing it seems to have become. It is one thing I am grateful for as a Romany Gypsy boy. We always ate healthily. Even when those ingredients were sometimes in short supply, or very basic. At least what we ate was healthy and wholesome. And I am reminded of the delicious stews Granny Lizzie would have simmering in that black pot outside her wagon. But look at the amount of eating disorders which seem to be commonplace today. Obesity, bulimia, anorexia.

Always start with a good breakfast. And I don't necessarily mean cornflakes, or those sugary breakfast cereals aimed at the children. Keep it basic. You can't go far wrong with weetabix, porridge, or muesli. But make time. Breakfast is the most important meal of the day after many hours without food. Give your body the start it deserves. Again, how many people do you know these days who skip breakfast to get to work on time. Take my word for it, it's a false economy.

Try to have three meals a day. Plenty of fresh fruit is readily and cheaply available. But try to make sure you have your greens too. Don't see eating as a chore. Find ways to enjoy your food. I try to cook as often as I can. I find it relaxing, distracting from everyday stress and satisfying. Better still, cook for someone else and make dining a positive social experience.

We are largely made up of water. It is an established scientific fact. So we do need to drink plenty... of water. Doesn't have to come in a fancy bottle, with an exotic name. Tap water will do. I have a friend who drinks nothing but coffee all day and wonders why he sometimes gets headaches. It's the excessive amounts of caffeine, which can dehydrate. Sure, he's drinking water with the coffee. But too much of anything is not good. It is all about balance. These days people are conned into low-fat this and ultra-skimmed that; low sugar, no sugar; low calorie, no calorie foods and drink. No calories? What on earth is the point?! I think we are fairly safe consuming most food and drink in moderation. And that includes chocolate and alcohol. Seems ironic though, when half the world has too little to eat the emphasis in the developed world is to lose weight. We have too much!

But, of course, now we have a binge culture. A total blow-out to excess.

To make us forget about our unhappiness for a short time? All these habits bring us dangerously close to addictions. Quick fixes in a society seemingly without any concept any more of maintaining balance. And look at how impatient we have become as we race from A to B in increasing amounts of traffic on the roads. Look at how stressed people are becoming. I have actually seen drivers banging their heads against their steering wheels at the first sign of delay in traffic. And now we have another crazy phenomenon: Road rage. People have been known to completely flip and kill each other for cutting each other up on the highway! What a crazy world. So pace yourself. Take it easy. Life is not a race. It's a long journey. At least if you look after yourself.

We've talked about feeding the body. But I am also a great advocate in feeding the mind too. We should never stop learning. It broadens our horizons and it really does sharpen the mind. Don't be afraid to take up a new hobby. It might be practical, or academic. But take pleasure from your learning. Take up something you perhaps always meant to and will enjoy. Sadly we are encouraged all too often to sit in front of the TV of an evening – that one eyed monster - and be drawn into an endless drudgery of soaps, or worse still, meaningless 'reality' shows. What a waste of time! If time is so precious, make the most of it. Sure, you can switch on the TV and switch your mind off every night, if you wish. Before you know it your life will be over. And what have you done? What have you learned? Except to become a couch potato!

Far better to get out and do something. Get yourself physically active, if you can. These days it is recognised that you don't have to go jogging for miles every evening to maintain physical fitness. They say 15 minutes of moderate to fast-paced exercise is all we need. Or walk more. Get a pushbike. You'd be surprised how many people will jump into the car to travel less than a mile to pick up a few essential groceries, treats or the daily paper, just to save time. Exercise is important for a healthy heart, circulation, physical stamina and mood.

But what about the soul? I've touched on it already. Make time to get away from the city and its hustle and bustle. Take yourself into the countryside and relax among the natural beauty of this green and pleasant land. Green is good. It's a fact. Green calms the body and makes the eyes dilate, especially the paler shades. Blue is also proven to have a positive effect.

Which is perhaps why it is so good to gaze up at a clear blue sky, or stare out across the ocean. Do switch off the mobile phone. No-one's going to miss you for a few minutes. You and they will survive, believe me. We somehow managed it before everyone had one. And breathe the fresh air! Slow and deep. Close your eyes and use your mind to create images. Think about all the good things in your life. And the people you love.

I certainly think it is important to consider what really makes you feel good. What makes you happy? Many of us work so hard that we forget how good it feels to paint, to sing, to dance and to create. We've mentioned cooking. Equally it might be gardening, getting your hands dirty, being outside and connecting with the earth. All of us have talents. They can be nurtured and developed. And these things help us express ourselves. In short, they are good for the soul.

Music too connects with our emotional side. Make time to listen and enjoy.

Nor do you need to be a maestro to sing along or a dancing queen to shake a leg.

Better still, seek out like minds. Spend time with your friends and loved ones, laughing and having fun together. Make memories and be grateful for the simple things in life which money just can't buy. These are the the real riches in life. And they all centre on caring and compassion, loving and giving, not taking. It's about being kind to everyone – and that includes yourself. And that brings me to another important aspect. Sleep. We all need it, but I guarantee, you'll sleep a good deal better if you take steps to keeping mind, body and soul in balance... and when you slip into a deep and satisfying sleep, dreams will come, taking you to places of unimaginable peace, beauty and fulfilment.

Chapter 22

Our journey together through the pages of this book has largely reflected on the past, my life's experiences and what I have learned. It has helped prepare me for what lies ahead. And I know each and every one of us is embarked on their own respective journey. Previous chapters have focused primarily on individual thought, and how each of us might view life, and learn from its trials and triumphs along the way. But what of the future collectively, for all of us? Where as a species and a sophisticated society are we heading in the months and years ahead? I don't think any of us needs that proverbial crystal ball to imagine what lies in store!

I would like to share a further story. This one's about the future. It focuses on our likely destiny and that of our children and our children's children. So it concerns all of us. Have you heard the one about the four horses? These are the steeds and the terrifying riders they carry with them, said to be unleashed before the apocalypse. Let me tell you, they are riding hard and fast. They herald the coming of Judgement Day and symbolise Pestilence, War, Famine and Death. And with the coming of the fourth, the Pale Rider, comes Hell itself...

It's a sobering thought. But if you are in any doubt, take a hard look at the world. There are signs that the calamities the riders carry with them are already in process across the globe.

The seven seals said to allow the horsemen into this world are being broken. So I'd like to imagine what might lie ahead if these shadows of the future remain unaltered, how we might be impacted... and the part we must all play to avert catastrophe as we move towards an uncertain future. It's a dangerous time.

Look at the rapid advance in technology which before long might overtake us, as artificial intelligence out-thinks, outperforms and outguesses the human mind. We are not far away from creating robot soldiers and war machines of unimaginable destructive power. Already scientists know that sophisticated computers communicate with each other and are calling for a halt on our ill-judged haste to develop things we do not fully understand. While we still can. We are on the brink of creating something we will soon be unable to control – and which might actually see us as a threat to be... terminated. Terminator Judgement Day! No longer seems so far fetched, does it? A frightening thought.

The world is currently more unstable than ever before, with epic power struggles and wars which we should have grown out of. Certainly after the horror and devastation of the first World War, when we first began killing each other on an industrial scale. It should have been the last time. But we haven't learned. Look how things have moved forward since then. The second World War was a further lesson. Men and women stood firm and united as evil threatened to engulf the world in darkness, and yet the Third Reich and its allies was defeated. A holocaust on a global scale was averted. But war and genocide continues with ever more frequency and sophisticated weaponry. Drone attacks kill innocents, destabilising countries and we see the vast movement of people fleeing conflict never seen on such a scale before, not even during the last world war.

Saddam boasted when he invaded Kuwait he was unleashing the 'mother of all battles' and he was ridiculed, seen as a tinpot, power-mad dictator from a country of limited interest or strategic value. But look at the legacy that ill-conceived Western intervention that was 'Desert Storm' cultivated and the rise of extremist terrorist groups across the Muslim world. That particular 'mother' has spawned spiralling conflict which has now spilled onto the very streets of London and all the major cities of Europe.

We have created the 'mother of all battles' through poor foreign policy dividing faiths, pitting entire regions, if not continents against each other. Rather than spreading words of brotherhood and trust we have created our own destiny through suspicion, hatred and self-interest – and this is what our politicians have done for us. But of course, there are vested, selfish motives. And we are back to greed. War is good business, worth billions of dollars. Is it any wonder then that the States and the UK have a thriving arms industry? And then there are egotistical maniacs with absolute power who seem intent on plunging the world into open global conflict once more. I am not sure which is worse. A crazy egocentric dictator in the Far East, or a trigger-happy hot-headed buffoon across the Atlantic...

Meanwhile climate change is accelerating at a rapid pace, bringing floods and storms of Biblical proportions. Who would have thought to see Texas, of all places, under water? Or millions evacuated from Florida fleeing the latest Category 4 hurricane. The earth is warming, glaciers are melting and natural disasters on an epic scale are becoming more frequent.

The signs of climate change can surely no longer be ignored and require globally co-ordinated action. Now. Surely we cannot turn our eyes away any more.

But I don't want to sound too bleak. We can adapt and make changes. It is not too late, but we must be quick about it. All of us have the power to make a difference. Yet at the moment we are all divided, with everyone out for themselves. This is the world we have created. Ask yourself: Will greed and selfishness create a better future for the generations to come? The world is slowly, but surely being seduced. We must wake up to our responsibilities.

People seem to be waiting for some great prophet to come again and save us, some super being. But consider, you are that 'super being'. Find the hero in YOU and become a strong warrior for your children, your family and your friends. And not in the latest computer game! I mean here and now, in the real world. Truth, justice and compassion will prevail if we all unite in the common cause for good. There is no need for hunger, homelessness, despair or war. But time is running out! We all of us share this responsibility for our time on this earth and will be judged accordingly.

Which brings me to another thought. And it links into Judgement Day. How we are remembered by others will be how eventually we judge ourselves. Our lives and our actions on this earth. Just as a farmer is judged by the crop he has produced. We should reflect on our lives and consider how our time will be seen through the eyes of those people we shared it with. In other words, if we caused suffering we will see our lives through the pain and suffering we have caused through their eyes. And we will feel the pain we inflicted, creating our own personal 'Hell'. Similarly, if we have created joy in those around us, we will feel that joy reflected back to us. This is how I believe we will be judged.

During this period of rapid advances in the things we can create and harness, we are still struggling to control our primeval instincts and are, to be frank, still very much behaving as if we were stuck in the dark ages. In many ways our technical prowess has overtaken our spiritual development – and our reliance on that technology may well become our downfall. Crops will fail, pandemic disease will strike, war threatens total destruction.

Next time the world comes into global conflict nuclear weapons will be widely used – and that could result in the annihilation of billions of souls.

Remember, though, as human beings we are created in the image of God, male and female. We are able to create life and also light to drive away darkness. We can all be strong enough to recognise lies and deception, to resist what we instinctively know is wrong.

And we can – we must – speak up for what we know is right.

Like Martin Luther King, I too share the dream. "I have a dream that one day... little black boys and black girls will be able to join hands with little white boys and white girls as sisters and brothers...

"I have a dream that one day every valley shall be exalted, every hill and mountain shall be made low, the rough places will be made plain, and the crooked places will be made straight, and the glory of the Lord shall be revealed, and all flesh shall see it together...

"With this faith we will be able to hew out of the mountain of despair a stone of hope... With this faith we will be able to work together, to pray together, to struggle together, to go to jail together, to stand up for freedom together, knowing that we will be free one day..."

Wonderful words which still send shivers along my spine. The great man may have been speaking for black civil rights, but in fact he was talking about human rights and freedom for all of us, regardless of colour, culture, or faith. And that's still very relevant to us today.

Have the courage to awaken from this false world we live in and become a beautiful person. The skin will get old, the body will age. But if you have love, you have beauty which people can feel. I am afraid the future does look dark, but I have great faith in individuals to unite and that we can change direction, urging our politicians to do the same. It's in our hands. We should not be led like sheep. Seek out the good in each other and not the bad; look to our common needs and desires, not our differences. Anger and misinformation threaten to turn brother against brother – all in the name of God. My religion is love. That's the common good. We are a small planet in an infinite universe – there are greater powers than us. So my advice is that we should make the most of what we have and not what we lack. We should surely strive to connect with our spirituality. That is where true contentment lies.

Have the courage of conviction to seek out those who will stand with you. That is where hope rests. In love and compassion, giving, not taking. And we should embrace it with all our might and all our hearts. The choice of how the future plays out is ours. We must grasp the nettle and make the right decisions for our children and the generations to come. I can see what is coming if we don't alter course. Yet equally I know how that destiny can be changed. So I will stress again, it is not too late. We each of us have the power to make a difference. Make the change in yourself first and radiate it out to the world.

Full circle

Chapter 23

My life started as a tiny, sickly baby born to Romany Gypsies in a small white caravan, pitched on that car park at the Horse and Coaches public house in a country village they were passing through. And look how far I have travelled. The road has been long. The Romany way may have vanished forever and I have spent many years as a *Gorgia*, a house-dweller, on a series of adventures and experiences called life. I have reached the age at which my father left this earthly world behind. I have laughed a good deal along the way. And I have cried too. Like all of us, life has presented a series of highs and lows that shape us into the people we become. Hopefully I have learned from experience and become a better human being, and have found meaning in life's rich tapestry.

Increasingly I reflect on my Romany roots, my time as a young boy on the road and the harsh, yet beautiful travelling culture that is such a part of who I am. The freedom I experienced in those early days and the influences on which I was able to draw have, I am convinced, given me a sense of enlightenment which is present in all those of Gypsy heritage. And I think of Granny Lizzie, of the stories that fired my imagination, of my father and his own trials, of my mother and how hard life must have been moving from place to place with four young children in such a confined space. But there was a sense of community, of being with people you knew, loved and trusted in all situations. I wonder what it must have been like for them, to see their way of life disappear. But I am grateful I was a part of it – and that I remember. Because I know it is in me and if I retain it in my heart and soul it will always live on.

Granny Lizzie was born in a bow-topped *Vardo*, pulled along the highways and byways of a changing, shrinking landscape at a slow and steady horse's trot. The world was very different place then. The industrial revolution was at its peak and with it came a transformation that was to change the way all of us would live our lives today. I am not sure all of those changes were good. Those swept along by dramatic social upheaval felt it then. Even when my grandmother was a girl the Romanies knew their travelling days would one day cease – that the nomadic lifestyle was nearing the end of the road. Granny Lizzie though was not so easily defeated. Nor was she tempted to give up her wagon. Not even when she saw her sons settle and become wealthy and successful. She could have lived a *Gorgia* life of luxury.

She was born in a caravan and stubbornly refused to abandon what she knew and loved.

And she died as she wanted to, in her beloved trailer. I wonder what she would have made of today's world. I can imagine her shaking her head and showing the lines of wisdom on her face with a knowing smile. We may have come a long way, but just look what we have left behind. I can almost hear her say it.

I hope I have learned along the way. I know I have made mistakes. But I look at my two children and the people they have become and I think I must have done something right. I have now lived many decades as a *Gorgia*, providing a house and a home to my two children as they were growing up. And

Proud of my Romany heritage

I have always sought to be the best person I could be, juggling being a single parent with making a rather unusual living, perhaps, as a psychic. In my personal and professional life I have always tried to cultivate the good in people. And that includes my own family.

Of course, being a lone parent has limited my own opportunities to travel, an urge never far beneath the surface of anyone with an ounce of Gypsy blood. And yet I have no regrets. I only need to look at the people my own children have become to realise the path that was laid before me was the only one I could have taken. And I have made the best of the situations as they unfolded for me. Both my children have grown and are adults now, with their own lives. The beautiful house in West Leake on which all my early hopes and dreams had rested for a happy marriage and family life was sold a few years ago. In truth, it was too big and expensive to keep and I now live quite happily and simply in a smaller property in Hathern, just outside Loughborough, bordering the beautiful Leicestershire countryside.

My son, James often works seven days a week building up his landscaping work and shows his own Gypsy spirit in his drive to be independent and his own person. He and his partner Abbie have two beautiful boys, Reuben and Beau, in whose faces I can see my own parents' features. So I am a grandfather! My daughter Katharine, who still lives with me, is a school teacher and has completed further study with distinction. Though we are still close in every way, I am certain she will be flying the nest before too long. Both James and Katharine have become loving, hard-working and confident young adults, and I am immensely proud of the people they are.

In this aspect of my life, I feel I have given all I could. It has not always been easy. Sometimes I have stumbled along the way.

But when I look at my children today, I know I did a good job, though many doubted me when they were still little. When I left the house at West Leake I decided to invest in a VW camper van. No horses required to draw it along, no 4x4 needed to tow a trailer. I have all the facilities I need onboard and, with my faithful Jack Russell and my harmonica I have company and music wherever I go on my travels, near and far.

So what have I learned along the way? I have learned not only to survive, but thrive. There have been tests, very dark times. But I feel I have risen to meet those challenges and overcome them. Sometimes it has been difficult. Yet always, even in the darkest of times, I had faith. Faith that love would win through in the end, as it always does to drive back the darkness. And I suppose the confirmation of the power of good has been reassuring. The trials have not diminished my faith, rather they have strengthened my resolve and my belief that we can rise above the tests that confront us... and win through.

I have also realised how little I know. As someone once said, the only thing I really know, is that I know nothing at all. So I want learn more. In other words, my learning has just begun. I have seen a glimpse of the magic and the power that this universe holds. My 'Gift' allows me to access incredible knowledge and wisdom that is channelled through me to pass on to help others. That, I believe, is my calling. To show others the way. I am not unique. There are others. And I believe all of us have the potential to unlock our spirituality and reach a higher state of enlightenment. We only have to open our minds and reach out unselfishly. I believe we can all be developed in the skills and knowledge I practice myself. Each and every one of us has the potential.

One of the central questions we will all ask ourselves from time to time is 'Who am I?' I knew from an early age I was a Romany Gypsy boy. I was different from most. I saw and experienced things as part of that travelling community that shaped who I am today. That life was not always easy. Particularly when I began to have more contact with the *Gorgias*, the house-dwelling communities. Settling down and becoming part of a different community was not without difficulties. I faced prejudice, isolation and suspicion.

Often I felt alone and that I would never be accepted for who I was, or indeed even if I wanted to become part of a community that initially felt very alien to me. I didn't feel liked, or understood. Sometimes I was even ashamed of who I was and where my roots lay.

And I felt I had to play a role that was not always comfortable, just to be accepted.

It has taken a long time to finally realise who I really am and appreciate what being a Romany Gypsy gave to me. In a word it is a sense of freedom. A freedom from the conventional. It is also a tough life, but taught me how to survive and adapt to changing circumstances from a very young age. It gave me a sense of independence, which has served me in good stead. But it also gave me an inherent a desire to travel, to learn and to experience new things. Today I am comfortable with who I am and, armed with the knowledge and experience as a mature adult, I am thankful. I know and have accepted where I come from, both the good and the bad.

When I look back on my travelling days now, it is with a sense of pride and fondness. Often still, I think of those days, moving from place to place as a small community, seemingly against the rest of the world, enjoying the freedom of the open road which was diminishing rapidly. Now it is gone. One rarely sees travelling Romanies. And yes, I do think of Granny Lizzie and the wonderful memories, the boundless love and the wisdom she shared. I know she sometimes still comes to me, just to make sure I am all right. I can feel it. And I am grateful for all the times she has watched over me in times of trouble. But most of all, I thank her for the 'Gift', which is a rare and precious thing. It is the gift of knowledge and enlightenment, which she saw in me from a very young age and nurtured. She was a truly wise and wonderful woman, my first mentor.

So I can today say with certainty who I am and rejoice in my Gypsy roots. And that feels good. In a way it makes me feel closer to those who have gone before. To Granny Lizzie, to my father, who passed many years ago. And to my mother, who reached the grand old age of 86 and retained her independence to the end. I also feel I know them better. Perhaps that comes with age and experience. You suddenly realise from your own pain and suffering what it must have been like for others to go through.

In this sense, I suppose life for me has come full circle. Today I am thankful for the travelling life I had as a boy and look back with a smile on those days – and realise the urge for me to travel again is strong. Now my children are adults I have the opportunity to hit the open road whenever the mood takes me, which is often, my camper van and I, exploring this beautiful country, making new friends, experiences and memories... and learning things along the way. I realise too, that I would be quite content to buy a small plot of land in the country, put a caravan on it and spend the rest of my days living simply, close to the land, travelling when I feel the need, which is how my life first began.

Looking back on a life that has been rich in both joy and sorrow, I realise it is not material wealth that we should strive for. It is for spiritual wisdom and enlightenment. This is the real reward on this journey called life to gather and appreciate. It is love, compassion. It is is giving, not taking. And just as Buddhists will tell you about karma, whatever you give with joy will eventually come full circle and return to enrich our lives.

Love is the answer. From my own experience I know it's true. It is confirmed whenever I look at my children and their children. Sharing precious times together, watching them, talking, laughing and playing, enjoying simple pleasures, bathing in love and smiles. That's surely what it's all about. I look at their faces and see in their features reflections of my mother and father. They live on. And I realise too the circle of life continues.

Ironically, perhaps, for a psychic, I don't know what the future holds for me. But I sense a new phase in my life is just beginning. Fresh, exciting horizons beckon. I know travel will be part of that life, as it must for all Romanies. It's in the blood. In a way, it seems the journey has been long, only to come full circle. I hope with a greater sense of knowledge and wisdom. But I feel at peace with myself and free. Free to hit the open road, meeting new people along the way and making new experiences.

One final thought. Whatever you do, wherever you go, whoever you meet along the way, always be true to yourself. They were words of wisdom whispered to me in love a long time ago, which I have held precious over many years. I wish you well on your own onward journey. Thank you for travelling along the road with me awhile...

What they say about Patrick

"I first met Patrick 10 years ago and only went to see him to prove that it was not possible for anyone to predict the future. I left with quite a different opinion.

Patrick has successfully helped me to make major business decisions, to manage health matters and to help with relationships with family and friends. Patrick has made a unique contribution to my life to ensure health, wealth and happiness."

Lesley Abley, Nottinghamshire, UK

"Normally I don't go for readings as I meditate regularly and feel I obtain the answers I need from my higher self. But when I visited the UK I was curious, from what a friend of mine had told me, having seen him.

Patrick and I connected immediately on a spiritual level – and he was able to tell me about my past and present. He was also able to focus on my husband and two sons. Very accurately. What a wonderful and amazing man!"

Daxa Chauhan, Toronto, Canada